How Not to be American

How Not to be American

Misadventures in the Land of the Free

Todd McEwen

First published in Great Britain in 2013 by
Aurum Press Ltd
74–77 White Lion Street
London N1 9PF
aurumpress.co.uk

Quotations from *Harvey* by Mary Chase are used by permission of
Josef Weinberger Plays Ltd.

Some of these pieces originally appeared in *Granta*, *Product* and the *Orkney Review*

A catalogue record for this book is available from the British Library.

ISBN 978-1-78-131235-3

1 3 5 7 9 10 8 6 4 2

2013 2015 2017 2018 2016 2014

Typeset by SX Composing DTP, Rayleigh, Essex

Printed and bound in Great Britain by
CPI Group (UK) Ltd, Croydon, CRO 4YY

This book is for
Seán Bradley and Fraser Smith
and for the People of the State of California,
who found not enough punctuation in my first book

Contents

Where there is no shame, there is no virtue.
OLD SPANISH PROVERB

Thoughts on the New American Uniform

I left the United States and came to Scotland just a few days after Ronald Reagan was sworn in as President for the first time. I had thought to escape what was obviously, already, going to be a Reagan 'Era'. And I landed innocently, but squarely, in *the Thatcher Era*. It would be fatuous for me to rehearse that for you – her creepy parroting of everything Reagan could manage to croak out about the economy, the plight of the miners . . . Denis Healey said it for us all when he got up in the Commons and called her policies 'sadomonetarism'.

After about ten years of this abuse I returned to my country for a lengthy period. And I found America, after all, to be sadly decrepit. The works of 'Reaganomics' were to be seen everywhere, not just in the lack of public services – in their grasping, selfish cruelty the people of my own state, California, had eliminated the irritations of taxes, schools, fire departments and public libraries from their lives at a stroke, in the name of 'tax freedom'. But there was a general run-down look to everything, everywhere: buildings, roadways, but more particularly the people. I thought for the first time that Americans literally have too much on their plates – there's a great *pressure to consume*, of course, but more than this, in the average Joe there's a toll-taking psychic dread about having to manage your life and also feel responsible for *world order* – something I realised I was happy to be relieved of as a resident of Europe. This of course before Tony 'Dr Moreau' Blair signed us up for infinite genetic experimentation.

For reasons too dreary to relate, I moved for a year to a remote spot in Arizona, near the Navajo and Apache reservations. My partner had a job and I did not, nor was I able to find any useful employment during the entire time we lived there. We lived in a tiny community whose only hope of survival lay in enticing people from Phoenix to drive four hours, 7,000 feet up into the mountains, to fish, golf, ski or gamble at the casino run by the White Mountain Apache. Naturally, you could get them to do this about once a year. The rest of the time my fellow citizens sat around on their mountaintop drinking and freezing – sometimes to death – in inadequate houses and trailer parks. In the depths of winter you went around wondering who needed the bait shops, gift shops, golf shops, tanning and nail salons.

Now, we have a thing called WALMART in America. This is a kind of combination McDonald's, Khmer Rouge and Vatican, a juggernaut emporium *and philosophy* which invades communities, first undersells the genuine, local merchants, kills them off, and addicts everyone to shopping in it. Personally I think they put something in the air. No one ever stopped to think if it made any sense to have a choice of fifty different kinds of television in a scattered community *7,000 feet in the air*. What would be wrong with going to buy a television in *Phoenix*? In this Walmart culture, everyone casually shops, all the time – they constantly hop in their cars for milk, lottery tickets, cigarettes, bait, and large guzzly cups of foul coffee. *Tea?* Forget it.

I was sitting in the parking lot of Walmart, wondering how I was going to feed myself, when I suddenly realised that everyone in the parking lot was wearing the *same thing* (except for me, of course, still ludicrously togged out in plus-fours and Inverness cape). What *they* were wearing was this: a baseball cap, a T-shirt, shorts, and what I was brought up to call *tennis shoes* but are now called running shoes, or in Europe, trainers. *This is what the poorest people on earth are wearing right now*, I thought. Reaganomics had foisted the third world upon us.

Everything we had seen, all the way from San Francisco to Los Angeles to Phoenix, and then all the way up into these here mountains looked so run down – the basic infrastructure of the country really was being ignored, because everyone (everyone who *could*) was having to work eighteen hours a day, thanks to what Reagan had done to the economy, *was still doing to it*. This is all the result of *the one Republican thought*:

> EVERYTHING IS A BUSINESS,
> THEREFORE EVERYTHING IS OK.

The more I looked the more I saw that this really was, and is, what everyone must now wear all over America, except in the

3

places which harbour harsh winters, when the shorts become jeans. Not that jeans will keep you warm.

A dreadful, overt conformism has surfaced in America, along with a real fear of each other. People used to enjoy being with each other, say at a baseball game. But now everyone in the ball park is afraid, afraid *something bad* will happen. Friendly rivalries between cities and teams have become real little wars, with their own terrorist outriders. Everyone's full of hate.

You can spot my countrymen in Europe by this uniform of T-shirt, shorts and cap. The American used to be spottable by a crisp new Burberry acquired in London and, as Fraser Smith once said, *a very silly hat*. And for my older fellow Americans this is still true – but if you get *underneath* the Burberry (yeccch!) this is what they're wearing. So I think of this now as a uniform – the *New American Uniform*. It has an important bearing on the world situation and how we may analyse it.

THE CAP

By the baseball cap, whatever it may say on it, Americans want to signal that they *are American.* But it is more a sign that they are part of the global marketing culture of fast food and pop music; it signals that they are *fresh from Walmart* . . . And you see everyone wearing this cap in every country now, on television, even in *National Geographic.* My definition of the word *democratic*:

= LOOKS BAD ON EVERYONE.

The root of all this is nostalgia – this cap is a quite traditional American thing, in the *old* way of it. It was worn, aside from people who actually played baseball, by newsboys and other rough but dependable lads. Look at old movies, look at the 'Bowery Boys'. The old felt baseball cap spoke *earnestness*, a quality which has disappeared from the American consciousness. An ancillary form of nostalgia may be seen in po-mo folk (as opposed to the mo' po' folk) living in places like Soho in New York, wearing hi-top sneakers and *genuine* old felt caps, which they get with that particular wasp-in-New-York ingenuity for obtaining the unobtainable: 'I really *am* living in 1957.' But these people have little to do with earnestness.

No one wears any sort of proper hat any more . . . the baseball cap was the casual, the populist hat in a world of real hats. Now it's more a *bra for your head*. With the New American Uniform you *have* to wear the cap, otherwise the head looks alarmingly small on the babyish, blimpy American body.

Baseball caps used to come in different sizes. I remember trying them on at the variety store when I was small. The advent of the *adjustable cap* was its aesthetic downfall. Surely this tab-and-hole at the back is hideous, the proof being when Americans of any age or either sex *pull their hair through the hole at the back*, or when they turn the cap around, eventually marking their foreheads in a way which makes them look like they've been whipped with a belt buckle.

'One size fits all' is global capitalism in a nutshell.

What about its uselessness as a garment? Skin cancer is now

epidemic, at least on the tops of fishermen's ears. Golfers suffer scorched scalps from the nylon versions of this stupid cap. In response to this cap bastardisation, baseball players changed *theirs*, which was very disappointing. Around 1975 they started wearing the hideous nylon mesh versions, more peaked, in the golfer/trucker mode, and then came the PUFFY CAP, made of foam rubber or something unspeakable. This was part of the McDonald's uniform for quite a while, though they've now gone back to a classier, smaller cap reminiscent of school teams. Perhaps McDonald's is wistfully trying to recapture *its* lost innocence?

Something cool was contributed to the cap scene by our blacks, who began to wear them in different ways – pulled round to the back, or way over to the side, the bill over the ear. This was meant to convey disrespect for the norm and was very effective – it was really a mockery of the cap and the larger culture.

Usually the cap (and the T-shirt) carry a commercial message or logo. This is pure cynical commercial tribalism, a plot of international companies to divide people. *To keep them from loving each other.* The rise of the New York Yankees' 'NY' baseball cap across the globe after September 11, in the light of their marketing tie-in with Manchester United, was deplorable. You now see these caps and other unathletic wear sported by the druggy myrmidons of Europe – if you needed further illustration of the identification of this cap with worthless media and drug cultures.

The meaning of this cap, to me, is a very sinister one now,

not at all to do with when I wanted to be a newsboy and say 'Gee whizz!' all the time.

Anecdote

Being someone raised by people who were roughly suspicious of mass culture, the hat *I* liked best as a kid was not a baseball cap but an olive drab army fatigue hat of the type worn by Fidel Castro, which led to no end of neighbourhood quarrels in southern California in 1960, although that is another story. The first hat I ever bought as an adult was a deerstalker – which I thought of as Holmesian but really only marked me as a lunatic in New York and, I suspect, even in Edinburgh.

THE T-SHIRT

T-shirts are UNDERWEAR. That is how we were told to regard them when young. So how's that for casualisation? My mother would never admit of a T-shirt being a 'real' item of clothing; they were also forbidden to be worn at school – and now they're the *basis* of American school wear.

The T-shirt is without complexity. It is like television: you don't need to bother with all that HISTORY, you can go out in the world in two pieces of cloth. A T-shirt worn with shorts reduces you to a PICTOGRAM.

The T-shirt is also the *ideal sweatshop product*. Thousands or tens of thousands can be made in an hour. T-shirts are now, like baseball caps, a medium for advertising. The shirt is *an external tattoo*. A T-shirt that had any writing on it used to be of course something you'd got for FREE – now people *pay* for the privilege of advertising things *for* giant corporations. Just so you know where they stand.

If you're wearing a T-shirt, your shirt tail is always out – the traditional mode of protest against school rules. The T-shirt battles with the Oxford shirt on the cultural horizon like Godzilla fought King Kong.

Women *eventually* started wearing T-shirts – but this seems to be about not revealing much of the body, the same as for men and baggy shorts – it's part of *the new prudishness* which has swept America, and . . . everywhere. T-shirts with stripes are particularly infantile. The Beach Boys wore stripy T-shirts – in fact an important association with all T-shirts, unless you are a French onion-seller, is summer, *endless summer and leisure*.

Anecdote

I remember a brown and yellow striped T-shirt I had when very young. This is a combination of colours I've avoided since. Again, my parents tended to look down on T-shirts as 'not real'. My mother's opinions of T-shirts are relevant because her thoughts on clothing mattered in the years that are being yearned for by people who are dressing in the New American Uniform. She preferred me to wear an absurd grey shirt with blunt tails, side slits and a little party horn embroidered on the pocket. So you see why I had to leave America.

SHORTS

always make *everyone* look stupid. Though I grew up in Los Angeles, and until I was an adult never experienced temperatures below 75 degrees Fahrenheit, I always had a horror of shorts. Especially the largely synthetic *tan* ones with an elasticated waist I pissed in time and again my first year at school.

People of my parents' generation *might* wear shorts at the beach but wouldn't have been caught dead wearing them on the street, into a store or a restaurant. But mostly at the beach the fathers were in trousers and the mothers in dresses.

The Bermuda Shorts Story. Bermuda shorts, real tailored ones made from suiting, came and went in the late 1950s and have never returned. The men in power in America today aren't going to show their knees to anyone. They are the serious ones, and if you're reading this, you are a kid with scabby knees. Wall Street is still suits. 'Dressing down' is for people without leverage. Dressing down is for people who work in Wal*mart*, not Wall *Street*.

But: The Development of Long Shorts. When I was a kid, shorts were short, shorts were tight. If I am not mistaken, long shorts (and loose) are another important African-American innovation. Perhaps basketball *has* contributed something to human existence? If you want a good laugh go look at basketball players of the 1950s or 1960s – their shorts were so tight that many a game was lost due to chafing or certain hairs being caught. So long shorts came in, and everybody was happier. But these loose, long luxurious silk-like shorts are also a denial of the suggestions of the male body. My wife says: *we girls are back to getting nothing.*

(There is a corollary here in the 'short-trouser mindset' in Britain, a sign the English in particular do not feel *citizens* of their own country. With the growing adoption in Britain of the New American Uniform, or maybe I should start calling it the New *Irrelevant Person*'s Uniform, this short-trouser mentality is reaching its apotheosis.)

Anecdote

A magazine cartoon: in American beach communities you often see this sign in a restaurant: NO SHOES, NO SHIRT, NO SERVICE. So there's this middle-aged couple, dressed decently, sitting in a restaurant under this sign. And the waiter is standing there wearing only shorts and he's saying to them: *Get outta here.*

TRAINERS

Tennis shoes? Gym shoes? Sand shoes? Running shoes? *Plimsolls? BUMPERS?* I was very embarrassed to have my trendy Green Flash tennis shoes called 'bumpers' at the beach last summer. I saw someone wearing them in *Vogue*, for god's sake. *Bumpers!*

Mom always said, *tennis shoes are bad for your feet. They give no arch support and they don't breathe. We don't wear tennis shoes in this family. TENNIS SHOES ARE NOT REAL SHOES.* But for some reason she once bought me a pair of PF Flyers – red – and I got a free whistle which looked like the moon. Like T-shirts, tennis shoes were never allowed at school, though some of the edgier characters in fourth grade wore them. This seemed goofy, or possibly seditious. It's possible, though, that these boys were merely poor. Tennis shoes STINK, but they can be washed in the machine.

That was *then*. But then came the Invasion of the Adidas, in the 1970s. And from that moment, tennis shoes got weirder and weirder and more and more hideous, to the point that they seemed actually to assert MENACE. Again, eventually, blacks customised the prevailing styles, which was to satirise them – walking around with the laces untied and the tongues hanging out – it called attention to the footwear of the ghetto (the third world – an important point), but was also like disobeying the teacher, having your shirt tail hanging out.

In the end, though, trainers are still a children's shoe. This gives the wearer the illusion of being engaged always in active play:

I DON'T WORK.

Let's be worldly for a moment: these shoes are made by very poor children in sweatshops – therefore in wearing them you say, 'I don't care who made this, it's the latest thing and I got it,' and this is really a statement that you're happy with the world the way it is, where we're to *accept our anaesthesia* so as to live happily with our GOODS.

The marketers need you to remain childlike – this uniform is proof that they are reaching complete control of our lives. They take the child as the model for the ideal purchaser – someone who is totally hypnotisable.

Anecdote

OK, I owned a pair of black Reeboks in the 1980s. So shoot me. My sister took one look at them and said, *Oh god, take those off! Black Reeboks are for rapists!* I got to thinking she was right, and for gym teachers – which were very nearly the same thing, at least in our town.

Addendum: SOCKS

Before the Revolution, you wore them pulled up to the knee. Then came the Period of Relaxation, or the Aerobic Era, and the advent of *slouch*. Since the beginning of the War on Terror, it's back to military tightness.

THE LAST STRAW: THE SCOOTER

Then came the little folding scooters. You began to see forty-year-old men pushing themselves along the street on these things, dressed in baseball caps, T-shirts, shorts, tennis shoes . . . The whole thing is too obvious. Where are the beanie caps with the propellers on top? *Where are the all-day suckers?* Everyone is being turned into 'Stinky' from the old Abbott & Costello show – a rotund, bald man of fifty who wore short pants, a broad straw hat with long ribbons on it and played with a stick and hoop.

Let's be disgusting for a moment: do you know what a *back-crack-and-sac wax* is? Ask at your neighbourhood salon. Men more than ever have got to be turned into hairless infants!

THE WHOLE MAN

The New American Uniform is clothing for CLONES. The human body requires *individual attention* to look good in clothes, which after all aren't natural. But this process is not about looking good – it's about being in an unofficial American *army*. It's about disappearing into a mass where you'll never stand out, never be seen again, and can't be targeted by those who wish to kill (or mate). And so you will live eternally! HA HA.

This uniform was in the 1950s and 1960s the uniform of *slobbering, fly-blown idiots* in *Mad* magazine and other comic books. See the art of Jack Davis.

'Sportswear', in general, is linked to homogenisation, tribalism, anonymity. Here we have the *idea* of widespread leisure, which can easily be shifted to mass idleness, not to say unemployment. A lot of people confuse these things already, unhappily enough for them.

The New American Uniform is a sexless outfit for men and women, though women seem often embarrassed to be wearing it; probably because men have forced them into it, into their army. We say these things, don't we, fellows? *This is the best thing to wear. It's real practical!* But it's a very bad look in terms of design, of dignity even, and it makes women look particularly bad. It is an anti-ethnic outfit, too. No wonder it is satirised constantly in the ghetto and the third world.

But American OBESITY is the real capper with this new uniform: they're all scooter-podging around wearing the baseball cap, the T-shirt, the shorts, and the trainers, and what does it say to the rest of us out here? It says to the world DON'T DEPEND ON ME – I'M ONLY A KID:

- I EAT HAMBURGERS AND WATCH TV AND CHEW GUM ALL DAY
- I DON'T SMOKE OR DRINK

- YOU *HAVE* TO BE NICE TO ME AND IF YOU'RE NOT I'M GONNA SHOOT YOU (*strapping on fanny pack or gun*)
- I WANT EVERYONE TO PLAY *MY* GAME
- I CAN'T UNDERSTAND A WORD YOU SAY

. . . and what is that but United States foreign policy?

Curse of the Sand People

The people of *northern* California always thought of their part of the state as green, as *lush*; whereas the Angelenos and the other accursed bastards who had to eke out an existence south of San Luis Obispo were trapped forever in a lifeless, dust-choked Martian nightmare *of their own making*. Everything wrong with L.A., and that was everything, was all their own fault, in our opinion. It began when they decided Hey, we could have a big fokkin city over here, and had to steal the water from the rest of the universe for pissing in and swimming pools but mainly the lawns, the lawns, their unending ubiquitous *LAWNS*.

But there were a lot of people in northern California who'd never been to school, who liked the stuff they had in southern California: freeways, smog, crimes, shopping centres. *Palm* trees? So they set out to DESICCATE northern California so that we would have to confine our existence to our cars, our houses, away from the smog, away from each other. They did this by stealing the remaining water and sending it down to the chumps with the lawns, and then by building up a city called San Jose (*without* the accent) which, though the venerable little farm capital of the

Santa Clara Valley, the 'Valley of Heart's Delight', say in 1880, became a frightening pseudolosangeles by 1960. From San Jose spread strip malls, hot rods, barbecues, trash, stupidity, dried-out lawns, garage sales and garage music, all through the northern part of the state. It was a giant denaturing decultivating wind which left everything in its wake dry and wrecked; it sucked up the topsoil of humanity and culture and never gave it back. Bad, hot, dry weather and culture then reigned in northern California, which had once been intimately picturesque with fogs, mists, real trees, bogs and so on. 'We' began to live what Stevie Smith called 'the tragedy of unwatered country'. Monterey and Carmel, which once depended on romantic fogs to draw visitors, now have to manufacture tons of cotton candy and bad watercolours, and build 'factory outlet malls', as without the heavy mists of the past, the cypresses of the Del Monte forest look scraggy and dried out. Which they are.

I may have been a fearful youth, but I wasn't a complete idiot. With that clairvoyance which turns out after all perhaps to be only coincidence, I could see that San Jose was going to overtake us. Not just with its weather and insistence on freeways and nothing to do in the world but shop, pig out and watch TV, but with its general grungy feel of rip-off houses and lives never got off the ground and people coming apart at the seams: life in L.A. and San Jose is what it's like five or ten years *after* they've Dropped the Bomb. That is its only educational aspect. O, tried to warn everybody.

As the traffic got worse, so did the weather. L.A. was seeping into our streets, our schools, our bones. I'm talking as if I give a damn about the town I grew up in. But as a fledgling enviro-paranoid I was filled with chagrin to see the verdancy and the waters of the place disappearing. Had to live there a few more years after all, before school and home could be escaped.

See, I dislike my town so much that I have gone back *twice* as an adult, to try to make a life there. *Went back*, yes, to see if I'd be . . . approved of? Or for a little more love? The first time I got so bored that I had to be rescued by friends from a major city which for legal reasons cannot be named. *What the hell were you doing?* they kept asking. *Quit your fooling!* they said. The second time I really DID go for love, for some *red-hot lovin'*, and too late realised my girl was ONE OF THEM, or had been infected by them – the Sand People.

I don't mean this in literal terms of the desiccation, the *mummification* of our part of the state ('most beautiful state in the union'), or that my girl had a POD with another version of herself in it, in the garage – social transformation in America just ain't that simple any more. My townspeople had always perceived Los Angeles and its satellites to be GARISH. San Francisco, a dead quiet place until 1950 (Harry Bridges the courageous longshoreman aside), always considered itself the more *respectable* of the two cities. (Bankers like to think they bring class to a town. Hoo *boy*.) So these snobs, these nanooks of the north, decided that they would have to look different from southern Californians, *even though they were already becoming them*, even though their water was already promised away and the dust of

San Jose's unculture was blowing up their streets in dense clouds. But their only defence of their realm was to *change their clothes* – they decided to start dressing like EASTERNERS. They affected pale blue cotton oxford shirts, khaki trousers, boating moccasins . . . my townspeople all began to look like snotty, seventeen-year-old snotty prep school kids from Boston. Did I say snotty? Partly because the local university was starting to *take seriously* its previously *jocular* misnomer, 'The Harvard of the West'.

These people thought they could *escape the tsunami of garishness* by becoming BLAND, by (it would seem in many cases) going bald, losing colour, growing mousy little moustaches – disguising themselves? To become dead-coloured, grey! They took their blonde hairs and cut them, they trimmed their insipid beards. But they were inevitably becoming the colours of the advancing L.A. and San Jose cultural desert. *Scientists later ascertained that this was fatal* . . .

1. Effect of sandy moustaches on doubtful-looking faces. Not faces of doubtful beauty, but that American, bedrock-Aryan face which constantly expresses doubt and suspicion.

2. Effect of rimless spectacles: to make freckled features even blander, less meaningful. More MOUSY.

As if everyone in my town knew, deep down, that they were in the middle of apocalypse, there appeared a new material anxiety, *the Ethic of Panicky Plenty*: mail-order (male-order?) catalogues from the suppliers of *sand-coloured clothing* began to be illustrated with STACKS of stuff: stacks of shirts, socks, trousers, sweaters – and my townspeople, who were now becoming *THE SAND*

PEOPLE, wanted to imitate this paranoid cotton harvest at home. Whole realms of businesses developed of closet reconstruction and enlargement and shelf-mongering. Like we were expecting imminently a special kind of world war, where there would be food after but not a sufficient or pleasing enough selection of *jumpers*. Houses became paler and paler on the outside; inside olive and terracotta began to rule with an authority they had previously only enjoyed around the Mediterranean. See? It was *happening*: everything had to become the goddamn BEACH. O, the white birch floors.

I was sucked into this; I had almost no frame of reference left becuz of the red-hot lovin' (and low wages). I found myself one day *arranging* some ORGANIC SOCKS I had been given as a present (if you want to look for PODS perhaps begin here), *arranging* them, *by shade*, in a drawer, not just *putting them into* a drawer. I was then immediately accused of being an *obsessive*. (All this was as antiphon, by the by, to the red-hot lovin', which didn't make me feel too good.)

Everywhere you looked, people and their possessions were getting paler and paler. It must surely be counted a signally black day in the history of western domestic ecology when people started to buy clothing that was already half washed away, half DESTROYED, by big *machines*, in the name of fashion, or to put it more bluntly, in the name of *making themselves disappear*. In the case of my townspeople, the wish to become wraiths in the tumble of the cultural onslaught, not to be noticed as American society crashed down about their ears. Real clothes don't even age in this way! I had to beg my girl not to buy any more sand-coloured clothing, for her or for me. It was a poignant scene, worthy of many a scary movie. But she would do it.

Dresses through which summer breezes blew, as if she didn't exist; colours that didn't change, or matter, with the time of day. At cocktail hour, everyone from her office looked like the familiar line of dead seaweed at the beach. My townspeople would never stoop to predominantly wearing T-shirts, but neither would they fully press their cotton button-downs: *we're not EXACTLY prigs, ya know.*

So you see how complicated, how hopeless. All these clothes and the people within them starting to fade away, with the incongruity of SHOES which won't biodegrade for 250,000 years – along with most of their other petroleum-partum'd junk.

The Parching of My Town

was on this wise – thanks in part to the Law of Californian Entropy which was enacted to ensure that *everything*, even Yosemite National Park, would eventually become part of Los Angeles; partly thanks to the local university which dictated paler and paler, more conservative clothing and thinking, in its wide-eyed, business-jabbering progeny. I was walking down our main street on a hot afternoon – I already knew the jig was up, but as a persistent, perennial FOOL I was hanging on, hanging in. I suddenly began to feel awfully ill. Dizzy as though the street were tipping from side to side, with tingles and even pain in my chest and arms. No, I thought, no no, I don't want to die in front of this *planter*, with its *hot bricks*, its *struggling succulents*, not here, not in front of the 'California Avenue Pharmacy'. For a moment I thought I must be having an allergic reaction to the brand-new carpet tiles in my brother-in-law's apartment – but then looking at the *succulents* I realised my gods, I'm in Los Angeles, it's GOT us. With this insight came no relief – everything started to whirl around and I saw that all would be swept away – the balding, the blonde, the tiny moustaches and beards, the light, light clothing, the rimless spectacles of the university, the pre-faded *chemises Lacostes* and jeans and all the spotless sneakers of California, all the Sand People washed out of their bare, sanded houses, all away in a great (and for them, gratifying) bleaching wave of L.A. nothingness, washed away.

A Trip to Ohio

Over the river and through the woods, to Grandmother's house we go!
The horse knows the way to carry the sleigh, through the bright and
drifted snow . . .

VERY STUPID OLD SONG

The first day that snowflakes started whirling around the campus, I dropped what I was doing and ran around ANNOUNCING to everyone that it was snowing. They were all from the East and didn't know what I was talking about. *Yes? And?* Naturally, being from Los Angeles, there were a lot of things I knew nothing about. Snow was only one of them. Snow, I thought, was literally light and fluffy as air and tinged a light sky-blue, around its edges – this was the only way it was depicted in the books we had at home. Once when I was five we managed to discover, on Mount Palomar, a patch of what my father said was snow. It was hard, corny snow which didn't give much, about four inches deep. Nonetheless I managed to lose one of my shoes in it and stood stock-still, one sock in this stuff, and howled my head off. This is still

23

the *only* encounter with snow ever referred to in the family canon.

When Easter came I had been invited to visit my high-school English teacher and her husband in Geneva; he was a physicist with a posting at CERN. It seemed reasonable to me, man of the world now after all – you keep moving east to find smarter and smarter people. I telephoned my father; outside all was deep grey; snow flurries obscured my usual view of the Triboro Bridge. Europe! he said, nobody's going to Europe.

I felt I had to go somewhere; everybody was clearing out for Easter, possibly the very strangest of holidays in America. I didn't want to be trapped like a rat in my dormitory for a whole week with only cheese sandwiches and cigars to live on. Somehow I managed to convince him instead to let me visit T, a friend from high school who'd moved to Ohio. I could fly to Cleveland and take a bus . . . it would all be dirt cheap and I wouldn't run into any *Europeans* or intellectuals probably.

Snow-cabbed it out to the white airport. Sat at the big blank windows, flew through snow and found myself in CLEVELAND OHIO early on Easter Sunday. Ohio means many things in my family: my mother's people were there for generations; the *Thurbers* lived there; some of my favourite toys were manufactured in Ohio; and I was so well-versed in the idea of Ohio that I would set up my trains to look like 'Ohio', even though I had never known what it *actually* looked like. Sometimes on Thanksgiving people from Ohio would come to see us. They all had white hair and were freaked out that the weather on Thanksgiving was warm in Los Angeles. Thanksgiving is one of those holidays that are *supposed* to be nippy.

I went from the airport to the bus station. All I could tell about Cleveland from this short trip in the snow was that it had a high part and a low part. The high part seemed to have houses on it and the low part was full of factories, railroad tracks and stuff like bus stations. For some reason I had grossly miscalculated my money – perhaps I'd paid more for my plane ticket than expected? – and did not have enough to go all the way to T, in Gambier. *Even though the snow was coming down very heavily outside the bus station in Cleveland, Ohio*, I looked at the ticket man and said, Well, how far can I go on *this*? – *and gave him all my money*. It made no sense, but I did it. I suppose I thought one just plunges ahead in these situations, though I am not sure that is my philosophy these days. I always head home if there's any trouble or it's after 5.30 p.m.

Bus through the snow, *thick snow with no money*. I was forced to get off in a place called either Wooster or Brewster. Or Rooster. There was a jam factory, and difficulty finding a telephone. I got through to T, who reported miserably that Gambier was snowed in; they wouldn't be able to come and get me for at least twenty-four hours. Do they have this problem in *Geneva?*

I had noticed, with a lot of *feigned indifference*, but now growing interest, that the bus had passed a place called Millersburg, where I knew my mother had people. So here I was, at three o'clock in an Easter blizzard, telephoning people I had never met for help, out of the blue. I'd had no expectation of meeting these people, ever

– possibly out of snobbery because of *Nobody's Going to Europe* and so forth. It turned out my family in the district were having *Easter Sunday Lunch*, and I mean with *capitals*, at the home of my great-aunt. My cousin didn't sound so much surprised as just glad to hear from me; he'd be 'right over' to pick me up! At my phone booth! Which meant he was going to have to put down his knife and fork and make a forty-mile round trip! In the snow! This was really perplexing. The guy should have hung up on me.

He duly arrived. Very hale, modest and kindly – we had a jolly trip to my aunt's house, trying to figure each other out, perhaps, while at the same time I stared out the window at the driving snow and at the Heartland, and realised this was the first time I'd ever really seen it. It seemed sedate, and powerful. As I listened to these relatives speak, whom I barely knew or knew *of*, who had magically collected me, I divined then that my father had somehow deliberately sent me here, into deep snow – he was afraid that I should only have experience of the *coasts* of America and, god forbid, people from *Europe*.

I felt I was an INVADING TWERP. But my aunt, too, seemed overwhelmed with surprise and gratitude to see me! We took off our coats and went to the meal I had interrupted. THERE WERE: baskets of freshly-baked white and brown bread, and of crescent rolls and of *biscuits* (in the Heartland sense). Tureens of cream of chicken soup and Scotch broth. Dishes of peas, carrots, beets, broccoli, Brussels sprouts, and potatoes mashed, baked and roasted and also a massive *potato salad*. This I was amazed and gratified to see. In my family potato salad was only dragged out on pointedly *informal* occasions; you would never give anyone *potato salad* in the *dining room*, or for *dinner*! What COULD you be thinking of? I was also pleased because living out of delicatessens in New York, between all that goddamn *intellectual drivel*, I could look on my aunt's potato salad as an urbane friend, well-met here in the Heartland. There were also a baked ham, and a HUGE CHICKEN. And a roast beef! *And three other people.*

My aunt poured herself a glass of sweet white wine – hers pointedly the only one. She had spent much of her life feeding and nursing my great-uncle, who'd been gassed in the First World War. This 'spread', as they called it, was the wonderful, almost unholy result of her skills. If *you'd* cooked all that in a day, you'd have a glass of wine, wouldn't you? Perhaps wine belonged mostly to churchy matters here in the Heartland.

I never had so much to eat in my life, not even at my grandmother's (whose rule was never to get up from the table before at least three of us were actually *howling*). Oh, then there were a few PIES: pumpkin, pecan, apple and cherry, each with the possibility of ancillary blops of custard, ice cream, cream, whipped cream or milk. This was literally stupefying; it was worse and more frightening than drinking too much beer. I have no idea where I slept that night but I can't imagine any of my relatives could have hauled my bloated and distended body into any car. I must have stayed with my aunt. I think so.

I won't tell you about breakfast, maybe you can imagine. Didn't this woman ever *sleep*? As I staggered around under the influence of hundreds of flapjacks, it transpired that T's road in Gambier still hadn't been ploughed, but my cousin offered to take me there. He had a small trucking business at this time, or rather was trying to rebuild it. Three years before, half his trucks had been washed away in a flood! These *floods* and industrial RUIN that are your thanks for living in the heartland. He was worried that I had no money for my journey, which was true – it was long before cash machines. Half his livelihood was gone and he opened his wallet to me.

My aunt's house was surrounded by the fields and barns of the Amish; she was one of a handful of 'English' who lived in their midst. I was raised to respect the Amish, as they were an important part of that Ohio we were always being told about. In our kitchen there were reminders of this as we grew up: a whatnot on which my mother arranged a very slowly-growing collection of Amish figurines, made of cast iron, by who I couldn't say. Surely the *Amish* have better things to do than sit around and mould replicas of themselves – like staying alive. They probably hold this kitsch in the same high regard they do radio and buttons.

After her husband died, the Amish looked after my aunt in many ways. The men made sure that everything in her house worked properly, and the women brought her the produce of their market gardens, vegetables and fruit. And, uh, *pies*. In turn, my aunt had a trough in her front garden which was always full of cool water for the Amish horses.

The Amish are often cruelly used now, both as symbols and in person, by the jack-fundamentalist TV-watching blimps who surround them. But in some cases they are starting to fight back – their young men are just as prone to take umbrage at an insult as any. Perhaps more so, as they really have a tradition and a way of life to defend. Not just their rights to certain television shows.

During the fifty-mile trip to Gambier, I had to reflect hard on the confused attitude I'd grown up with as regarded 'family obligations'. My father was always scornful of the fear I felt towards my cousins. His idea of countering this was to threaten me that if he and my mother were killed in a car crash or struck by an *atomic bomb*, my sister and I would have to go and live with those people. It didn't work at all – my sister and I quickly agreed on a suicide pact should this come to pass. Much later it came out that my father couldn't stand some of his relatives either.

In my cousin's car, his daughter talked at such length about *proms* and other social matters, that the Heartland began to seem more alien than when I was safe on the bus or being stuffed with food. My own high school, in a spirit of flailing radicalism, had eliminated such bourgeois trash as proms and student government, a year or so before. So I wasn't sure if I ought to relate to her enthusiasm. Arrival at Gambier! Hearty goodbyes from the relatives I had never seen before and would never see again. Their unquestioning kindness and concern for my welfare had me puzzled for a very long time. *I* must have appeared to them like something on a peculiar UHF television channel, in the middle of Easter.

Gambier is a college town. The word *college* had always

summoned to my mind a picture exactly like the place I now found myself: tree-lined, slightly hilly streets, gracious frame houses, so on – and I thought again that I had never actually been in such a place before, my childhood having been spent sleeping in dumpsters and furniture stores – ach you know what I'm trying to say – SUBURBIA! – and my own college urban, without the traditional trimmings of Campus Life. No barbecues, no cheerleaders. And here was T, my friend, who had moved away from our town four years ago. One of the real trials of adolescence is such a separation – just at that time when everything in your head and your body is out of control, and HURTS – from someone you expected to be a fixed buddyroo. But can two eighteen-year-olds actually *reminisce*?

Politics

T and I had both become interested in politics at the age of fourteen or fifteen – this led us to spend time in a tired old office building downtown. I doubt whether such an office building would be allowed to exist now, or if this one still does. The last time I was there, in my old downtown, I guessed it had either been torn down and replaced or covered over with a MOCK ADOBE look, as though they were ashamed of it . . . perhaps it's just the usual Californian shame at anything over five years old. But what made this office building unusual, maybe even a SEDITIOUS BUILDING, was that it housed in its time the local campaigns for both Robert Kennedy and Eugene McCarthy, an extremely dangerous left-wing newspaper, and the local branch of the National Association for the Advancement of Colored People.

T was of a more confrontational bent than I, and he ended up working for Kennedy and hanging around the left-wing newspaper, where he picked up a lot of zeal for stopping the development of the area, and got an interest in photography. Believing that the meek would eventually inherit the earth I plumped for McCarthy. And since I had *heard* about black people, I worked for the NAACP, answering their quite silent telephone several days a week. We had lots of leaflets in stacks, though few people called at the office to ask for them. I also got involved with a peace group, the Concerned Citizens, who were in a small rented house nearby, but that was more because it was a place where I could practise my banjo on Saturdays while selling little CND badges. Badges, posters and stickers ('79% of your Federal Tax goes for WAR!') were in large part our politics.

Nobody in or out of the NAACP seemed to find it weird that a white kid (I) was answering their phone – when it rang – and handing out leaflets on housing discrimination. But most everything in our town was done by white people, which was a big problem, maybe *the* big problem, in the first place. I don't mean they were running the NAACP, far from it, but somehow the fact that *I* was fronting the office of a Saturday signifies for me a certain confusion in the liberal thinking of that time. I knew a couple who joined everything, they were at every meeting of every group devoted to reform, *in their sandals*. They were white, they were in the NAACP, in the Concerned Citizens, they were part of a movement which opposed downtown development (this failed utterly, though it took twenty-five years for our downtown to be fetishised and boutiquised into something even the crass developers of 1968 could never have dreamed of – a desolate land of expensive Italian restaurants, a town where you cannot buy a HAMMER or a NAIL). This couple contributed photographs and articles to the paper T worked for, they participated in demonstrations against the local right-wing think tank (a morally bankrupt, shamelessly marketed department of the university, actually). All in these *sandals*.

In a weird way, these *sandal people* were the precursors of the *sand people*. But where sandal people acted, the sand people merely shift a little, like lumpen dunes, or blow away (preferable).

In retrospect it sometimes seems strange, all this *sandal energy* devoted to solving 'problems' in a community which, to almost the entire rest of the human race, would not seem to have many. The prosperity of our town gave a surreal hue to humanistic thought to say the very least, perhaps has destroyed it by now. Under the surface, it was never a free-thinking place at all, the economy underpinned as it was, and is, by computer makers and defence contractors.

It was quiet in the NAACP office on Saturday mornings. Occasionally I would close the office for a few minutes and go down the hall to the newspaper to see if T was there. If not I'd go back and look through the neat pile of *Ebony* magazines, most of which were several years out of date. *Ebony* was a photo-news magazine like *Life*, except for black people, which is odd, that black people didn't figure in *Life* – no, of course they needed their own magazine! I'm not sure that *Ebony* satisfied, it always seemed to be trying too hard. But in it you could read about a few people you'd only vaguely heard of, and plenty you otherwise would never have heard of at all.

There was a very attractive old typewriter in the NAACP office and one day, completely at a loss for something to do, I wrote on it one of the most useless, naïve pieces of journalism ever conceived: 'NAACP: DOMINATION IS NOT GOAL'. Thinking to hand it in to my school newspaper, dispatches from the front line of area politics . . . I think I was hoping to inspire instant, non-frictional racial harmony in our stifling, stifled town. Really by hanging around the office *alone* and reading *Ebony* I had learned nothing about the immediate racial situation. I showed this production to the man who chaired the local branch, an astute, kind man named Stanley. He read it over, smiled, and kindly, discreetly, put it in his pocket.

Kindliness was the characteristic of the NAACP people I knew; no doubt this was seen as a failing by those in less patient, and possibly more effective, groups at the time. One of the kindly older men in the chapter wanted me to go to church with him. At first this seemed a good idea – we'd meet outside the church, then as he put it, we'd 'go in to worship together'. Thus making a statement. The church was a white church, I needn't add, near my house. My parents' jaws hit the floor when I told them where I was going, of course, it had been a long time since I had *been a priest.* In fact I don't think I ever managed to astonish them to quite the same degree again. But when I got to the church I couldn't make myself go in! My mistrust and fear of religion got the better of my desire for racial harmony.

I was a paid-up member of the NAACP and as such was the possessor of a badge and a sticker. Without asking (natch) I stuck the sticker on the front window of our house. (I *thought* of it as 'our' house.) This caused a real to-do in the family. My parents apparently felt that having an NAACP sticker in the window (or maybe it was just *any* sticker?) would lead to our house being attacked. But by whom? If they were afraid of some kind of imminent race war, wouldn't our house have been *protected* by this proof of brotherly love? So went my reasoning. So they must have been afraid of *white* people clocking the sticker and burning our house down, which was even weirder, given the kind of people they generally were, sandal wearers, or incipient sand people who never do anything. Then who, who? Door-to-door brush salesmen? But door-to-door salesmen had always been *banned* in our town, one of its many attempts at a hoity-toity superiority over the rest of America. But the fear and disgust grew and grew at the dinner table until I was asked to take the sticker off the window, which proved rather hard to do, the *sticker* of course having assumed its job was to make a permanent show of the family's convictions.

But this sticker must have had magical properties. On the very afternoon on which I succeeded in acetone-and-putty-knifing it off 'our' window, a very strange, rare black man came to the door. He wanted money, claimed to be collecting for a charity, but had no identification or *informative brochures*. Which you were supposed to have in our town. He had a theatrical, antique way of talking. I couldn't figure him. Our dog, an enthusiastic, loud, cowardly sort, came tearing towards the front door as I stood there wondering how to deal with the odd man. Our dog's barking and snorting (put on no matter who was at the door) caused the man to go into a contrived and, to me, offensive show of Being a Black Man Afraid of a Dog – I've never seen anything like it – 'Oh, Sir (!), he doesn't like black meat, does he?' – accompanied by pantomimic hand gestures and the most alarming grimaces. I didn't have any money and eventually I gave him a box of matches and some loquats. This performance pissed me off and really confused me about the racial situation in our town for a long time. I wanted to ask Stanley at the NAACP about it but I was scared he wouldn't believe me.

Perhaps in such an artificial place, relations between any group and another remain artificial. Theatrical. There is a six-lane FREEWAY that neatly and perhaps permanently divides black from white in our town, divides them with noise, ostentation, pollution. (Has always *most conveniently* divided them.) But I know two black men on the white side of town today: if they go anywhere at night, they get stopped by the cops. *All the time*; pulled over again and again, often by the same, recognisable cops. These are both men with careers, families, both notable former athletes. Again, and again, and again. Black guy in a car!

Politics and Playboys

See, there were other reasons to be downtown. *Nat's.* Nat's was immediately downstairs from the NAACP and the radical paper and McCarthy and Kennedy. Every town worthy of anything at all has, or had, a Nat's: a fluorescent-lit pookyhole in the wall filled with magazines, things almost like pathology exhibits in smeared jars (black twist? liquorice rope?), a large humidified Lenin-like cigar sarcophagus ('Serve-Ur-Self'). Nat's was open early in the morning till late in the night. *Far* into the night, for our town. It was run by men with the egg-yellow eyes of the cigar aficionado, cigar *addict*, in golfy trousers and little pot bellies. The *Racing Form.* The *Police Gazette.* An Ali Baba's cave of pornography, in our town of large, beautifully kept houses, daily swarmed over by army-ant gardeners; houses like resplendent, indifferent mistresses.

It's amusing that the Sand People, the university people more or less tacitly admit the need for tobacco and smut, the partners of an intellectual existence; you see lots of them in Nat's all the time. Not everything is *completely* repressed in our town, they just make it tinier and tinier until it fits.

Nat's was not unknown to us: my father would occasionally smoke a cigar while drinking an Olympia beer on the patio. He was talented that way. He wasn't a secret smoker; he wasn't a hearty smoker. But once in a while he'd have a cigar on the patio, or (dangerously) out among the dry hills (near water of course). If he smoked in the house my mother puked.

Several years back ownership of Nat's was transferred from one pair of golfy trousers to another. The new trousers said they were keen to preserve Nat's as a little institution of some kind, its 'family atmosphere'. I almost fell out of my chair. Some family atmosphere. Any family that based its life around Nat's would be a prize: they all smoke like chimneys, even the pets. They live on candy and 1,000-year-old beef jerky. They take no exercise save turning the pages of hundreds of magazines about baseball, skiing, windsurfing and snowmobiling. In fact it's a wonder that it's a family at all, since when the strip lights finally go off in the wee hours they all retire to bed and ferally masturbate amongst Nat's journals of the flesh. My high school English teacher once broke off in the middle of a lecture about *Julius Caesar* to tell us, apropos of nothing, NEVER to go anywhere near Nat's, never to have anything to do with those *evil men I BEG OF YOU*. She was really worked up about it. Kind of cute.

Our town had another side. Although they have all but vanished now, there were traces of a Not Nice Town. We were all paper boys. When you are a kid your life takes place at home – it's only when you start getting erections, and a little money, that you discover 'downtown'. My introduction to downtown was Lev, who had the paper route there. To fill in for Lev on his downtown paper route was dirty and sexy and dangerous, we were all dying to do it.

Behind the main street there was a place called the Chester Hotel. The street level of the building was leased out to other businesses, you entered the hotel through a single door: CHESTER HOTEL in old gilt letters on glass. The way no one can make signs any more. You were immediately on a steep staircase, and then found yourself on a dark landing, in a sinister world of black rubber runners. The hotel was probably of the same date as the radical office building. Flabby men peered out of half-open doors, scratching their stomachs. An ancient Not Nice Town smell of regrettable things fried on electric hot-plates, beer and the sweats of beer, cigars and cigar spit. Lev said that walking up into the Chester was like walking up into somebody's ass. Here there were two or three customers for the paper. All these men looked like Carnival People, Who Were Bad People as we had all been thoroughly warned. I beg of you.

Across the street from the Chester was a 'card parlour'. Its windows were completely painted over from the inside with lettering offering

POKER

PAN

LO—BALL,

the only card games allowed in our town, because none of these is much fun. The State of California thinks they are games of *skill*, not *chance*, so they're legal. And 7-Up! Offered in the same aged sign paint, sure, why not, live it up, blow your brains out! This place had a name, but nobody knew what it was. We called it the Lo-Ball, and that was its name in Lev's account book. The smell of the Lo-Ball, when the door was open, was that of old air conditioners choked with a million White Owl cigars, warm beer, urine and pants. The men sitting around in the Lo-Ball never looked up when you went in and put the paper on the bar. They didn't look depraved or ill like the men in the Chester, just tired and out of step with the times, like people you see at the track – pork-pie hats, cheap sunglasses, spectacle-cases with big clips in their pockets.

A lot of *these* guys lived in another hotel, the Red Bird. The Red Bird really was a hotel – that is, it had a lobby and a cigarette machine and a desk with a sleeping man behind it. It had its own barber shop (formerly an American tradition) with faded pictures in the window of stupid-looking haircuts on thick guys who looked like they wanted to look like Tony Curtis, bent cards of plastic scalp-massage brushes on the walls, and a little black wire stand with faded jars of butch-wax on it. All the *Playboys* were five years old, scarily over-handled, and when you opened them a lot of various hairs came down into your lap. The barber had a lot of moles on his face and he gave you the same haircut no matter who the fuck you were or what you said: Regular Boy's. If you were Yves Saint-Laurent or the President of the United States you'd walk out of there with the plucked white sides of a Regular Boy's. He treated everyone's head like it was a chicken. He gave me an inappropriate squeeze once at the conclusion of my haircut and I had to avoid him, or walking past his shop, for years. I mean I am still having to do this, he's still there.

You Shouldn't Hang Around Barber Shops. You Should Just Go In and Get Your Hair Cut and Pay the Man and Leave, Because You Might Hear Something Improper.

In our town now most of these places have been supplanted by art galleries, post-modern Mexican restaurants and hot cookie stations. It would be impossible for a place like *Louis's* to be there, a decrepit hobby shop where Lev, this other guy Hollenius and I bought the tracks, fake trees and rolling stock for our putative cooperative *model railroad*, so you see how far back we are going now, how pathetic. Louis's was stacked from floor to ceiling with dusty model kits. There were only one or two lamps in the whole place and since Louis only sat and chain-smoked all day the windows were stained dark. His wife was a brittle, sallow woman on whom a lifetime of Male Hobbies, passive smoking and twelve-year-olds had taken their toll. To my surprise, Holennius once brought her a rose. Mrs Louis used to wear very bright lipstick and the rose matched her lips as she looked at it sadly. Later when we had the fight which broke up our railroad consortium, I shouted at Hollenius that he'd given the rose to Mrs Louis because she looked, in a way, like a girl he was hot for at school. This drove him into a rage.

But the place that really excited us, the reason we all wanted to fill in for Lev, was Mary Ann's Kountry Klub, a tired wooden bungalow of the 1920s, painted beige, several blocks away from the un-nicest part of Not Nice Town. It was on one of the two streets, near the railroad and the bus station, which always smelled like diesel, even in the middle of a spring evening. To deliver the paper to Mary Ann's you had to go in the back door, into the kitchen, where you found a surly chef surrounded with institutional-sized cans of *lard*. Every dish in the place must have been made of lard. When you went into the dining room and saw Mary Ann, you'd believe it. She weighed three hundred pounds. She wore black tent-dresses or gypsy-type robes with a lot of crappy jewellery and lardings of violent blue and purple eye shadow. This place was a whorehouse, only we didn't quite get it at first. It just seemed bizarre: there were a lot of little tables, at which couples were sitting. The girls were all wearing cheap dresses, cotton dresses like you'd buy with trading stamps. They were chubby and moony. The guys all looked like Bud Abbott: sharky suits, thin greased-back hair, rat teeth, rat moustaches and rat eyes: what were guys like this *doing* in our town? You never saw them on the street. It was as if every icky-looking shoe salesman from the 1940s had been rounded up and slimed down a chute into Mary Ann's. Where did they live, what did they do when they were not in the Kountry Klub, 'romancing' these girls? The Buds held the girls' hands across their Blue Plate Specials and sneered at them. The girls fluttered their eyelashes at the rat-Buds, doing bad impressions of Ruth Etting. Their nails were garishly enamelled and they wore little white flat shoes with pointy toes.

So when I went into the subversive office building, off the busy main street, it felt like stepping through the tailors' shop in *The Man from UNCLE*, from the workaday world into a network of intrigues those outside knew nothing about and were POWERLESS to stop. And now you see how successful we radicals were: everyone of consequence got bulldozed or assassinated; pollution is 1,000 per cent worse and everything has been developed to the point of meaninglessness and ruination; everywhere there is war, absolutely everywhere. Everyone is now practising war. Back then we were making war on our parents, we had to, that was a large part of our politics. It's a shame we never escalated that war generally.

But T did: parents can have their own plans and dreams, can't they? Even though it's 1968 or so? T's did and they moved the whole family away out of California and into the Heartland, where as practically the only liberal, not to say *radical* kid in his new school, the only kid with BOOTS, T ran amok, had to be 'disciplined', whatever that meant, and was generally supposed, with his *mimeographed newspaper of shocking ideas*, to be a grave threat to the entire State of Ohio. He wrote me very long, unhappy letters in those days and I couldn't see what good it was doing him to be there, in a place where no one would listen. It was a shame and a waste for society.

Many years later, T visited me. He had married an ecologist, a pretty, smart, capable woman, a SENSIBLE Ohio Girl to whom I took immediately. She and I had some long discussions on the state of things and found we were in complete agreement: the pursuit of profit was just about to put the finishing touches on ruining the world. Just a friendly, casual conversation of the kind you have around the barbecue on the Fourth of July, Independence Day, which it was. Being that we were in Aberdeen, Scotland, the day was wretchedly dark and cold, laughably so really. We'd been sitting in the park with our picnic, hoping the sun might come out. I can't think why we didn't go to my house, only a few streets away – it was probably American perversity: on the Fourth of July you have to picnic, goddamn it. It doesn't matter if you are at the bottom of the Marianas Trench or screwing around with a fake flag on the moon – picnic, you crazy, freedom-loving bastards!

In the middle of our jolly, recreational doom-mongering, which suited us environmentally paranoid types down to the ground, and also suited Aberdeen, a world doom-mongering hot spot, I suddenly became aware that T was *seething*! He'd turned pale, paler than the weather had bidden him; he was suddenly very defensive, afraid that his wife and I were going to destroy the western economy for the sake of some what, ideas? *Birds?* Just get up from our picnic and turn the switch off everything everybody'd worked so hard to build – I could scarcely believe this, given his politics in the past. (Wrong of course to assume that people don't change; but T's radicalism had always been one of the benchmarks of my own attempts at politics, and a crucial aspect of the way I remembered my adolescence. There had been a *fighter* or two – T was one of the main reasons there was any discussion of Vietnam at all in our school newspapers, rather than just guff about basketball, grades, *getting ahead*, and Career Days where a bunch of drunks would show up, boast about their jobs, and ogle up *our women*.)

I had forgotten that being stuck in Ohio, say being stuck in the Middle Of It All, where all is blandness and fear, that listening to all that bullshit, and it is, can really change you eventually, even if you're a smartie!

I heard Wynton Marsalis interviewed about his work for survivors of Hurricane Katrina in New Orleans, his town. He was asked how he was able to find out what was going on, who was safe, who was missing? He said that there's no way of getting the news, the truth, in his country any more. 'It's all theatre,' he said, very ruefully.

OR – it's possible that some dubious HEARTLAND THERAPIST had convinced T that 'the radical politics' (*his* phrase, talking disparagingly of his younger days) had been a maladjustment of some kind. Anyway I found that T had been replaced on the political spectrum by *me*; this was uncomfortable and weird. T was in fact an independent businessman, surrounded by the landscape of Babbittude; he was beginning to parrot it.

As if in some kind of official Pathetic Fallacy Nightmare, it began then and there on that Fourth of July not to *rain* on our parade, our barbecue, but to *hail* on it. Could any three Americans have been any more unhappy that day? Huge, hard, *painful hail stones* the size of golf balls. This bombardment seemed to underscore my isolation and changed feelings (here in the vigorous weather of my adopted country); what a long way from home T and his wife suddenly felt. We were the *picture* of disconsolation.

I've lost at least two 'comrades' (yes I'm using this ironically) in the course of my life, T and also K, who despite being a musician, a talented instrument-maker, a university graduate, a lawyer and a father, thought that making war on 'Somebody' after 11 September 2001 was a very good idea. Anybody.

Ohio Girl Makes Good

T's wife bears an uncanny resemblance to another Ohio Girl I know, who lives in New York, also pretty, capable, sensible, smart, always on the right side. Loves her country. They could be sisters . . . perhaps they are, on some acerbic Roz Chast moral plane, where they all wear the *narrow capable eye glasses* of the Heartland. Frankly, I like knowing women like this; they make me feel that all is not lost to astronauts, businessmen and politicians. If they're still capable of understanding me and if we agree about the way the world is going, then I haven't left the world, Europe, and gone all the way on to Left Field or Mars.

After the presidential election 2004 Ohio Girl went quiet for a while. She was depressed after having knock-down drag-out fights with her family about George W Bush. Living in New York or any other part of the real world, of course, there seemed no earthly use or good to the guy; in Ohio for *undisclosed reasons* they felt exactly the opposite. At any rate they saw fit to deliver us into his unhorny hands for a second vexing, embarrassing, destructive four years.

When Ohio Girl could at last bring herself to speak about what had befallen the country, without giving voice to her astonishingly pure, piercing Heartland scream, straight out of the finest drive-in horror movies (something she normally saves for Hallowe'en or when icky men follow her home from the subway), she rang me up. She said she had but one desire in the aftermath of the election. This was to go to a nice ordinary American pet shop, purchase the most ordinary collar and leash, invite the President over for Hawaiian Punch and canapés, get him on the leash and lead him around her Ohio Family's ordinary basement rumpus-room, kicking his ass every few seconds, in the nicest possible, most ordinary way. 'I've never really thought politically before,' she added, hurriedly.

So, you see what happened in a Republic regime to our simple, sweet, pretty, sensible, smart American girls? What she thinks of Obama, her saviour, and his more than tacit approval of torture, rendition, drones and spying on simple, sweet, pretty, sensible, smart American girls just like herself, I'm too scared to ask.

On Not Being Jewish

When I was a child, everything swayed me. I had not access to any art, any thought, anything good – for the society the family found itself plunked down in was one predicated on the miserable, tired, post-war ideas of niceness, sameness, sanity, prosperity, ignorance and hypocrisy. The suburbs. So if I evaluated anything, it was from the point of view of the nice: how nice is this? Nobody died, or if they did they died in OHIO. Nothing particularly bad happened at home. The worst thing that happened at school was mathematics, or Tony Carrison twisting my arm behind my back. And if that's the worst of your schooldays— .

I felt that I could participate in everything, subsume everything (except mathematics), that everything was there to partake of, and understand. When I was quite small I conceived no objection to going to church, even though our church was hideous, the music terrible, the minister a droning ineffectual bully. But it was a SHOW of some sort, and that was what I liked: SHOWS. (Everything a medium.) There were also a few things to ponder: how did they keep the red candle suspended in the apse constantly lit? Mother said it must never go out. But surely . . . Why was the altar sacred, and where did the sacredness end? Here? Or here? I enjoyed watching my mother kneel, pray, find a hymn in her missal and sing it. She seemed to know all about this stuff – where did she learn it? Yet more stuff you were already supposed to know.

What I didn't like was when she announced that from now on I'd be going to Sunday School – taken away from her for half the service, sent with a lot of DOPES in party clothes into a fake classroom, where two awful ladies immediately set about torturing me with what I didn't know and was *already supposed to know*. They never *taught* us anything, these awful ladies, they just asked questions and then humiliated you for not knowing the answer. It was 1,000 per cent worse than the worst day at school. Granted, maybe I was supposed to be reading some passages in the bible during the week, the Hell with *that*. No way was I doing *homework* for something that wasn't real. (I only liked what was real. Spacemen yes. Cowboys no. Got tripped up about *pirates* which I early assumed were not real.) So I stopped even trying to answer the questions and would only immediately say DON'T KNOW and stop my ears to their cackling imprecations. All I could think about was my father, at home, mowing the lawn, and how nice the back yard was on a Sunday, and how my church shoes from JC Penney were *killing* my feet. Endless singing of hymns you were already supposed to know; endless colouring-in of thrilling scenes from Judaea.

It was a relief to go back in for the final part of the grown-ups' service. In our church the ritual was pretty stripped-down, being across the street from a supermarket, but it was there, and for a time I was fascinated by it, and set about trying to understand it by imitation. Altars have wood, wood and flowers, I reasoned. It was hard to find anything made out of wood in our neighbourhood, but in the garage I came upon the empty cabinet of an ancient record-player/radio. It had holes inside where previously there had been knobs and vacuum tubes – these could hold glasses of water in which you could put flowers, so I dragged this thing into my room. I was always dragging dirty things into my room. I went out to the back yard for churchy flowers, though all the family could ever grow were geraniums, ugly little things that they are. I didn't recall ever seeing *geraniums* in church. But. I opened the lid of the cabinet and put the flowers in. I put on my BATHROBE over my clothes (vestment). I didn't have any organ music among my records, but *The Sorcerer's Apprentice* seemed appropriately THREATENING in parts so I put that on and started doing priestly things, I can't remember what – waving my arms about symbolically. Dad came in. 'What are you *doing*?' he said, 'are you a priest?' I had to admit that I was. Yes, I was A PRIEST. I'm not sure if that was the *exact* day he started reluctantly shaking his head in contemplation of me . . . I only wanted to help him mow the lawn, but I was bored and corrupted so here I was staggering around in a robe to Paul Dukas . . . I think this is how most people become priests anyway. Slaves to ceremony; the most hapless unwitting victims of SHOW.

I later reclaimed, *deconsecrated* my room for SCIENCE, as a *planetarium*, thanks to my Dad. Same music though.

The bathrobe incident was embarrassing and I began to hate going to church at all. A year or two later I flatly refused to go. This was perhaps the greatest mistake of my life. You face your parents across the breakfast table, the power . . . Yes, the feeling that I had WON was shortly dashed – forever – by the annunciation that from here on we would not be going regularly to church BUT that As A Family we were going to read the bible together every Sunday morning. We would read the whole entire bible, including the parts that no one has ever read, start to finish. My father said he estimated it would take 500 years. In fact I think it took us three or four years, during which time we moved towns and I had got just enough education in me to start being a real weisenheimer about the whole thing.

For four years every Sunday I sat in my pyjamas in the large red Naugahyde armchair, feeling my bottom getting very sticky and hating absolutely everything in the world. My mother read her passages in a weird, movie-style religious voice which really gave me the creeps and made me feel she'd been taken away from us. My father read his like he'd read the Yellow Pages, only occasionally evincing interest or making fun of somebody's name. *Abednego* he found particularly funny. My sister's style was one of abject terror. I read out my bits in the worst, pain-filled monotone I could. I also refused to answer any questions, it was just like Sunday School! But there's no winning against PARENTS, parents who've decided to STICK TO SOMETHING even though it is ruining their lives too. When we finished reading the entire bible I was thirteen, and was learning in school about the Bhagavad Gita and the Upanishads. I suggested we ought to read them next. *Fine*, said my father defiantly, knowing I was trying to get back at them, to force some crap down their throats. And we did, or we started – it fell apart pretty quickly because none of us of course could work up any enthusiasm for the Upanishads.

The other religious problem in the family was my uncle, a real know-nothing zealot who'd gone nuts on Jesus because of something weird that had happened to him in the Army. My aunt and my uncle dedicated their lives to torturing us with religion whenever they could. For birthday presents they sent bales of badly-illustrated sub-biblical trash. When we got together on vacations my parents would go out to lunch with my grandmother and my uncle, leaving us alone with my aunt and their two kids, already doctrinaire fundamentalists of the worst water. Can you imagine trying to play Cowboys and Indians with someone, a *kid*, who constantly draws you aside and demands to know if you have asked god into your heart? (Actually, it's possible that life on the frontier was like that, because there were plenty of religious maniacs running around. But *still* – !)

Like most zealots my uncle was also a prize-winning egomaniac. He spent years of his life writing his *own* scriptures – 'THE DEUS SCROLLS' – the 'word of god' wasn't enough for him, he had to wade in with his own finger-in-the-dyke additions and amplifications! Like *Tolkien*, that daft old twit for whom the real history and languages of the Middle Ages were not enough.

Do these guys never stop? He also set up his own church, which was about worshipping HIM, and, for his disciples, eventually supporting him in his dotage.

For a 'religious' man my uncle had the most profound and neurotic fear of death I've ever encountered in anyone. So what good was his faith doing him, let alone us?

After we moved towns I got to know some Jewish kids and in the manner of my priest-play I was briefly SUBSUMED in what I knew, or what they would tell me, of their religion. My friend A lent me his textbook from Hebrew school. It dawned on me that here was a religion which I could use as a valid slap in the face to all the Christians and their rubbish I'd been forced to endure. The next time my cousin came at me with his questions, I held up my hand and said, 'Stop right there. I feel it's only fair to tell you that I am *secretly Jewish*.' This had the desired effect and I had the pleasure of actually watching someone I despised *slink away*.

The first little drips of racism I was exposed to came from my very lovely grandmother. When I was very small I was fascinated by our mail man, a tall, very friendly man who always had a kind word for me. I knew there was something unusual about him but attributed it to his height. He seemed – I use the word in retrospect – *iridescent*. One day my grandmother noted my friendly relationship with the tall mail man and drew me aside. *Those kinds of people are called coloured people, and it's not good to have much to do with them.* That's always the problem, isn't it? Someone you love poisons you. I was perplexed, staggered; though I rarely felt I should question anything my grandmother said, because I loved her so much. So I rather doubt I questioned my parents about her strange assertion.

But I think now, my desperation over the black/white question when I was a 'budding radical' aside, the bigotry that has had the greatest effect on my life has been anti-Semitism. The summer after we finished primary school together, and were 'looking forward' to junior high school (what a mistake!), A and I attended a 'Day Camp' at the school we had just left. 'Day Camp' is a stupid, cheerless idea – you sit around on benches, locked out of the classrooms you know only too well, and mostly make 'arts and crafts' projects (= crafts projects) under the direction of *very* bored teenagers hired by the town's recreation department. There is no swimming, no game-playing. You SIT, staring out at the green playing-field. We took a full week to braid some blue and red nylon threads into a thick cord to which a key ring was attached – this was supposed to be something you took home and gave to your parents, to impress them. Proof you had been *out of the house* and not attacking someone or getting washed away in a storm drain. I had already planned to bin mine before I even *got* home, knowing well my father's reaction to everything that was hideous. On the last day of Day Camp we were waiting outside the school for A's parents to pick us up. There was an older kid, a lug, who'd been casually threatening to beat A up as long as we had been attending Day Camp, so that was another of its glories . . . As we waited there, the lug approached us and took up a threatening stance in front of A. He grabbed his key ring, called him a dirty Jew and said he'd get him one of these days. A bristled, in astonishment, fear, fury – perhaps at this moment our ride came. I don't remember anything happening except sitting in the back seat, next to a weeping A. What's wrong?, said his father. That guy called me a dirty Jew, said A. The reaction from the front seat was impressive: a totally silent wave of hot astonishment, anger, and compassion. This was immediately followed by a calm, reasoned explanation by A's father that this was going to happen, either from time to time or a *lot*, but he hoped very seldom in A's lifetime, but that when it happened it had to be met with dignity – and firm resistance.

I knew I was witnessing something important in that car. I knew that they would rather not have had me there at that moment, but I felt a part of it nonetheless, and empathy for my friend – the hurt he had received, and, apparently, the hurt that was to come. I wonder if it figures as largely in his consciousness today as it does in mine.

I do not know if that incident (and my incipient sympathies with anybody who is not Christian) propelled me more towards Jewish friends, but as this was my first palpable, semi-adult confrontation with prejudice, since that day I have been (perhaps too slowly) becoming more and more aware of the ubiquity of anti-Semitism. If I analyse it carefully, I have to say that, yes, almost everyone I have known, in any walk of life, in any place I have lived, has at one time or another made anti-Semitic remarks. The more I think about this, the more frightening it is and the more hopeless I become. It can wake me in the night and convince me I have to flee all this unfairness, all this inhumanity. But – ah – where?

'Jewishness' is one of the hearts worn on the American cultural sleeve – compared to where I live now, practically on the Roof of Europe, where who is Jewish and who is not is a matter of some secrecy – and, therefore, of resentment. Jews have made the greatest contributions to American life. And it has been odd to come to a place like Britain and to realise that this vital human spark has for the most part to be hidden. You haven't experienced a certain exquisite kind of human squirming until you have heard an Englishman drop *sotto voce* into the conversation that the proprietors of such-and-such a supermarket ARE JEWISH.

Who the fuck cares? You want lettuce or not? They taste terrible, don't they, those *Jewish* corn flakes? Drop dead, ya wanna drop dead?

The Big Three

> *Yes, America is gigantic, but a gigantic mistake.*
>
> FREUD

Several years ago I taught some writing and literature courses in a small (religiously-based) liberal arts college in the South. (It's worth noting that the word 'liberal' in this sense is now the cause for some shuddering and shame – there was in the Reagan and Bush era a collective erasure of memory of what the term 'liberal education' actually means.) I wasn't teaching Southerners only – they were well-meaning, 'B' students from all around the east coast. I might mention that not one of them had read a full-length novel in high school – this is not done any more; Dickens, Faulkner, Ellison are encountered only in excerpts. Of course their vision, their *meaning* must fail to impress in this way – they're understood only in terms of how their work is described. So that is very depressing and difficult for a teacher, like teaching cooking by showing juicy photographs of steaks and pies.

We were required to inject some classical drama into our patients – if I *could* have done it by hypodermic I would have – yet they enjoyed *Oedipus Rex* once it got rolling, as who does not. One morning it occurred to me I was being remiss in not having said something about the relationship of Freud's work to these characters and situations . . . Practically as soon as I'd opened ma mouf I realised that none of these people had even *heard* of the Oedipus Complex, let alone Freud, let alone contemplated the motives, urges or scenarios, the necessary feelings and problems Freud described, only for our benefit and enlightenment. With *every word* I got myself in deeper . . . Some of these people were *nursing* students, surely they had taken some psychology? . . . eyes widened by degrees . . . I felt like I was hawking red-hot wienies at a briss. To put it mildly. To suggest this kind of thought about adult sexuality, about our natures, was literally anathema here. And, I thought later, as I plunged my entire head into a sink of ice-cold water after class – *Jewish*. The more I thought about it, here was something wholly missing from their culture – not only the achievements of Freud, but, I discovered, also those of Marx and Einstein. The culture of this school (it is not the only one) and the cultural lives of these young people were literally untouched by the texts or even the *spirits* of these three Jews. Creepy: like looking something up in the redoubtable Eleventh Edition of the *Encyclopaedia Britannica*, wherein you may read a perfectly reasonable, recognisable account of the world until it dawns on you that this also is a world without much electricity, telephony, without flight (and also without Freud and Einstein, needless to say). But maybe it's as much a problem of illiteracy as it is Christianity . . .

In the novels course I taught, which I *at first* facetiously titled 'Worry in the Twentieth Century', Plath, Beckett, Bernhard, some of the most skilled, beautiful commentators on what a pass we have come to, fell on deaf ears. My students simply couldn't be convinced (or cajoled or even *threatened*) into viewing life as a problem, let alone tragically, even as an intellectual exercise which might, just might, get them somewhere. 'Why are all these people so negative?' 'Why dwell on these kind of problems, what's history got to do with being alive?' 'This guy's mentally ill.' I would sit there and feel the three most important Jews draining away from the world, everything was becoming colourless . . . Nice. Everything had to be accepted as it was, certainly no criticism of society, large or small, could be of any benefit – for Americans everything is graven in stone, it seems. They could not be induced to see the rich artistic ground, accepted for centuries, by a comic, self-abased brooding on one's own foibles and fate. Nothing is going to change or be allowed to change – 'that's the way it's always been done around here'. When you visit America you should be prepared for the idea that the young, of all people, are completely hidebound. Recent generations have been given nothing, except a kind of TV-illustrated corporate world to live in and look forward to. Faced with my students, I felt like lighting a cigarette and cynically reaching for the phone like Philip Marlowe calling the cops in front of the bad guy: *Think it's time we had some Jews in here, pal.*

Einstein: 'When you are courting a nice girl an hour seems like a second. When you sit on a red-hot cinder a second seems like an hour. That's relativity.'

Pretty un-Christian; measure the universe? Ask yourself why you are the way you are? Question the hideous social mechanisms men have made in the name of wealth and progress for oppressing, killing each other? Nobody in America's going to listen to Freud. They think he's dirty. So we're dead. And we're dead too because they don't listen to Einstein ('I don't know how they will fight World War Three, but I'll tell you how they'll fight World War Four – with sticks and stones'). And they don't have to listen to Marx any more because they've conveniently forgotten that socialism is democracy.

Sartre wrote that if the Jews hadn't existed 'we' would have had to invent them. *But not in Carolina* – they're tooling along quite happily without the three most important Jews in the world. O if only I could have left that place at the speed of light.

I had little to do on my weekends there in the South, except to try to locate a martini (alcohol is strictly controlled by the state, available only in garish, shame-inducing Hell holes) and to watch a very pleasing combination of dark clouds and rain which looked white against them, and the deep red soil on the banks of the river, the trees in spring flower – it was all very familiar, reminiscent of a picture book version of Joel Chandler Harris I'd had as a kid. One of the professors – he'd been raised in this town, travelled to Europe for his degree, and now found himself back here, a little dazed and perplexed – invited me to visit some of his relatives 'up in the hills' on a Saturday. So up through all these admirable, pungent, nostalgic colours. If you have never seen the hills of the Carolinas, direct your motor car thither. Thing is: keep a-goin'. Telling you.

His cousins and uncles lived in a number of tilty, cobbled-together houses, and constructions somewhat less than houses, in several clearings at a high elevation. The collection of dogs, car parts and the extracurricular junk of rural life exceeded expectation. These were people on the edge, who had no sense of edge. Mostly illiterate, they survived by hunting, poaching, and regularly stealing from each other. Women were not much in evidence. When somebody needed 200 dollars to buy a crappy car which he needed to function for a week or so, he took a job on the railroad. These were some of the most relaxed, open and hospitable people I have ever met. Spray painted on the houses round and about were religious slogans: Jesus Loves You, and, most frequently, OBEY GOD. Down in the college town (though it was really more of a saw mill, giant trains which keep you awake all night town), which already seemed another planet, there was a television channel dedicated to showing church services that featured brave SNAKE handlers. Well the snakes were putting a pretty brave face on things too. And in the same town there were big Baptist churches where women in pastel dresses lushly sang hymns and abjured snakes ah *declare*. They really say that stuff.

Having almost nothing, the professor's uncles were very open-handed. They gave us some meat and began handing round large tumblers of moonshine. It was distilled from pears. It was heavenly, and when I awoke in the strong sunlight of the mountains the next morning, in approximately the same position on the porch I had been in when I took my first sip of this nectar, one of the dogs happily licking my face, I was staring directly across the road at one of the shacks:

OBEY GOD.

Incredible; no *infidel gin*, but *this* stuff. Karl, *I found* the opium of the people. You'd love it.

The dog's name, incidentally, was 'Obie', pronounced like 'Toby'. **OBIE DOG.**

As we descended the hills later that day, I said to the professor that in all fairness there ought to be a Moonshine channel and a Refreshing Face Licking Dawg channel in addition to

SNAKE CHANNEL. Because of the moonshine, some of this is guesswork.

A Breather

Any religious talk now sounds to me like bullets coming out of the mouth. Bullets and blood. In the past I told myself it was only polite – *polite!* – to respect those who have religious beliefs. Heck fire, in ma banjo-playin' days I sang lustily the bluegrass gospel. Now I can't accept it, can't touch it, can't stand to hear it. My reaction to religious faith has hardened to one of total despair. I have a friend – a Muslim – whose compassionate, practised, gently articulated faith still impresses me, but it doesn't touch me as it used to. I formally apologised to my mother once about all the bad things I'd said about Jesus, whom she still admires in some weird way. I said it once and I wouldn't again. I wish he'd leave her alone.

If I had any power, not as the paltry, easily deposed little despot I propose myself elsewhere, just the power to suggest things and be heard . . . if I were the Secretary-General of the United Nations, the chairman of the World Bank, the head usher at the G20, the president of the European Commision, the President of the United States (but who listens to *them* any more?), Hell! if I were the *Pope*, I would call for a world-wide moratorium on religious faith. For a year? Ten years? What is a generation? During this period I would ask every man and woman who professes adherence to a religion to stop to examine it. What is your religion telling you to do? If it and those who lead it advocate harm, cause harm to other men and women, go to your scripture and see if that is what is actually required there in the 'word of God'. (You might do the same with your stock portfolio.) If your faith really does require the invasion, rape and destruction of other peoples, it is time to think. Ask yourself if these popes and mullahs and wizened, worm-like archbishops, these guys screaming themselves hoarse on television, guys with SNAKES, even the plashing, pastel choirs, aren't driving you INSANE and asking you to waste your life in hate. Proposing to ruin your life as their tool in ruining the lives of others.

You could stop.

The religionists' most powerful argument, it would seem, is that if we eliminated 'faith' we'd be left only with television and McDonald's. But these things are successful only because they *mimic* the degeneracy of religion. America didn't *have* to throw ten thousand years of civilisation out the window. It didn't have to abandon real education and a just, circumspect place in the world. Those things are under dire threat from the adrenaline religion brews in us, to hate, to gloat over swathes of others. But they could be regained, rebuilt during and following the world's RELIGIOUS BREATHER. It's not too late. Even a minute's peace would be worth it.

On Two Twentieth-Century Greats

MICHAEL JACKSON

1. Extensive facial remodelling.
2. Pinched, unnatural 'waxy' look.
3. Sleeps in sealed glass chamber.
4. Crowds queued for days in order to see.
5. Electrifying dance style.
6. Rounded up and kept thousands of animals in private zoo.
7. Inspired fanatic loyalty.
8. Likeness available on hundreds of products.
9. Insisted on being called 'King of Pop'.
10. *Thriller* second biggest album in history.
11. *Thriller* is 13-minute horror video.
12. US schoolchildren voted him best hero of 1980s.
13. Had sister's nose (mail order).
14. Signed biggest record contract in history.

V. I. LENIN

1. Extensive facial remodelling.
2. Pinched, unnatural 'waxy' look.
3. Sleeps in sealed glass chamber.
4. Crowds queue for days in order to see.
5. Electrifying oratorical style.
6. Rounded up and kept thousands of people in prison.
7. Inspired fanatic loyalty.
8. Likeness available on hundreds of products.
9. Insisted on being called 'Father of the Soviet State'.
10. USSR largest nation in history.
11. Term of office was 13-year horror.
12. Russian schoolchildren voted him best hero of 1900s.
13. Had father's eyes.
14. Signed 3rd largest number of death warrants in history.

The Lion of Democracy

As normal Republicans justifiably expand, their enormous energy-chomping children need to be housed. This requires the building of vast preternaturally ugly homes in natural environments previously untouched by normal Republicans. This means contact with life forms normally unseen by normal Republicans, and some ugly incidents have already occurred in this area. Democrats may venture from time to time into normal Republican areas seeking water or food.

TO: HONORABLE CITY COUNCIL
FROM: CITY MANAGER DEPARTMENT:
                POLICE
DATE: MAY 24, 2004 CMR:284:04
SUBJECT: SUMMARY OF THE DEMOCRAT
                INCIDENT

This is an informational report and no Council action is required.

Background

Early in the morning of May 17, there were several sightings of a Democrat in the residential area around Rinconada Park. After searching for the Democrat for about seven hours, the Democrat was observed jumping over a fence on Walter Hayes Drive. About an hour later, the Democrat was located up in a tree a short distance away. In the interest of public safety, the Democrat was shot and killed. Since then, there has been a significant amount of misinformation, speculation and rumors that have resulted in hundreds of people contacting the City and Police Department. The purpose of this report is to provide the Council with an accurate and detailed account of the incident, the chain of events, the resources the Police Department consulted, and the rationale that led to the shooting of the Democrat.

Discussion

On Monday, May 17, at 4:45 a.m. the Police Department received the first call from a person delivering government-sympathetic newspapers reporting a Democrat in the 500 block of Coleridge Avenue. The Democrat was hiding in the bushes. After attempting to determine the validity of the call, officers initiated a yard-to-yard search. At 5:40 a.m., two residents reported seeing a Democrat in the area of Cedar and Parkinson. He was seen running down the street. In light of the fact that there were two very recent Democratic attacks on polls in the lower foothills and due to the fact that a predawn sighting of a Democrat in a highly normal Republican neighborhood is extremely rare, there was great concern for the health and safety of the community. A field command post was established in the parking lot of the Palace of Terrible Art on Newell Road. The on-duty police lieutenant assumed the role of Inquisition Commander and began making requests for assistance.

Contact was made with the Fire Department Battalion Chief, Political Services staff, and the Department of Homeland Security. By 6:00 a.m., requests for assistance had also been made to the County Department of Political Health Vector Control, which responds to calls about mosquitoes and Democrats, and the Downtown Young Normal Republicans. The U.S. Air Force responded with a Stealth fighter, but due to the nature of political thinking in the city, which exists as a sort of fog, it was unable to strafe, bomb or nuke the Democrat.

Because staff knew that schools in the area would open soon, the Superintendent of the School District was contacted and advised of the situation. Staff's primary concern in the early morning hours was the safe, ideologically sanitary passage for children walking and riding to school. Staff took up fixed posts at key locations near the schools, watching for any signs of dissent or free speech.

To better understand the potential danger of a possible Democrat attack and the scope of the problem facing the community, staff relied heavily on political experts for information on Democrat behavior. Staff learned Democrats are the largest number of native voters. Democrats are known by a number of names including wise-ass, knee-jerk, cloud cuckoo, spendthrift and bleeding heart. They are primarily nocturnal, shy, elusive and solitary, except during the convention season and when young, are often seen traveling with their mothers in Volvos. They are agile fence-sitters and are very fast over a short distance, say a term of four years, but because of a small lung capacity, can almost never be heard. They hunt at night and while Chinese food is their favourite nourishment, they have been known to prey on sushi, Thai food, sophisticated pasta and even normal Republican hamburgers and beer. Adult male commute ranges often encompass more than 100 miles. After the mother gives birth, the father loses interest, goes crazy and splits. The mother raises her young alone and trains them to vote. The young stay with her for up to 18 years and then disperse to college, commence voting, and then come home *again*.

The Democrat is classified as a specially demonised mammal in California. The California Department of Fishy Seeming People may remove or take any Democrat that is perceived to be an imminent threat to public safety or thinking.

Staff consulted political experts from respective agencies about the alternatives to subduing and capturing Democrats. Contact was made with the police chief of Morgan Hill, Captain Morgan Hill, in order to determine how it recently handled three Democrat sightings in that city. One option that was explored was the use of a tranquilizing agent. Staff learned chemical immobilization is used for capture purposes only under very controlled circumstances (such as when the Democrat is balloting) and that many factors must be considered before even attempting to tranquilise a Democrat. In most cases it takes anywhere from 20 to 30 minutes for the chemical to take effect. During that time, Democrats may become agitated and are usually mobile and have the ability to jump from position to position, and can be highly voluble. In some cases, the tranquiliser has no effect. In Morgan Hill, it took six shots of José Cuervo to subdue the Democrat. However, the tranquilizing agents available in the City Police Laboratory normally constitute Wild Turkey and Budweiser.

There will be occasions when the initial anesthetic agent does not provide adequate immobilization or when the effect of the anesthetic agent begins to wane before the Democrat is able to be captured. In these cases, there is heightened danger for all normal Republicans in the area. Oftentimes the Democrat is startled and immediately takes off running. It is impossible to predict where a Democrat will run or what behavior he will demonstrate. As the Budweiser starts to take effect, a Democrat may become more confused and more defensive as he loses control of his wards.

At 12:10 p.m., staff initiated the process of activating the City's political alert system. Before the system could actually be activated, however, due to the fact that staff had *initiated the process* of activating the system as opposed to activating it, a fourth sighting was reported. At 1:05 p.m., the Democrat was located asleep in a tree at Walter Hays Drive and Walnut. Officers observed the Democrat and a request was made by the officer to shoot it. At that time, a considerable number of news media, and also normal Republicans, were in the immediate area. While an officer present at the scene was in possession of a tranquiliser gun, based upon the information noted above that attempting to tranquilise the Democrat could create an even more dangerous situation for the public, the order was given to shoot the Democrat with a lethal round. While the Democrat was not at that moment ready to campaign, as has been reported by left-wing newspapers, this action was taken due to the Democrat's inherent threat to the community by being in a heavily normal Republican residential area. Because the Democrat was in a tree about 15 feet above the ground, a very safe, not to say *hugely attractive*, trajectory of fire existed, up and away from surrounding beautiful expensive homes and important normal Republican bystanders. Officers quarreled briefly over the honor of killing the Democrat with an AR-15 rifle equipped with an advanced normal Republican 'no foresight' system. This uses .223 caliber intangible information that breaks up upon impact and is less likely to be identifiable and therefore politically damaging. At 1:06 p.m., a single shot was fired and the Democrat fell out of the tree. It ran for several local offices, fell over and was pronounced dead at 1:07 p.m. No other shots were fired and no political or ideological injuries or damage to some of the city's most impressive and costly homes was reported.

The Department of Homeland Security took custody of the Democrat and transported him to Roswell, New Mexico, where a necropsy was conducted. The results of the necropsy revealed that the Democrat was a 150 pound male, 30 years old, slightly politically underballast, with a stomach overly full of White House crap. There was no indication of rabies. But many Democrats are rabid. The bullet hit both lungs and the heart. The Democrat's ability to travel any distance after being shot was most probably the result of a high level of adrenaline in his system. Democrats are usually full of fear, whereas normal Republicans are not. According to the pathologist who conducted the necropsy, the location of the shot, the heart, which bled, resulted in the most predictable death. While it is unfortunate that this Democrat had to be killed, it is important to emphasise that police staff made the decision lightly, with much joking and good humor.

Since the incident, a number of additional questions have been asked including the following:

Why wasn't less time allowed to elapse before shooting the Democrat, even though it was sleeping and up in a tree, seeing that the primary election was only weeks away? Staff wanted the option of laughing and joking about Democrats, if possible toying with the Democrat, and enraging him. But they were conscious that they did not want to take the chance of allowing the Democrat to escape again or worse, politicise a person on the ground. As noted above, an attempt to shoot a moving Democrat would have significantly jeopardised the safety of every luxury vehicle in the vicinity.

Why wasn't the community alerting system activated to warn residents? At the time of the initial sightings, due to the few number of officers on duty, the focus was on getting normal Republicans out of the area. After the third sighting, the focus shifted to erecting ideological barriers around the schools. The arrival of left-wing news media resulted in staff responding to their stupid liberal questions and taking them out for coffee and lunches. With all the associated brawls, staff did not think of activating the system. In fact because nobody knows what it actually is, they are authorised only to think about initiating the process of beginning to activate it.

Are there any more Democrats in the area? Since the shooting of the Democrat, there has been only one unsubstantiated sighting of a Democrat, on television. There have been no other reports.

How was the Democrat able to travel from the foothills to the residential areas undetected? Staff theorises that the Democrat traveled through the shopping mall, disguising himself by buying as many up-market consumer goods as a normal Republican.

How will the Police Department respond in the event of another sighting or incident? If there are reports of any additional sightings and officers are able to determine that the report is credible, a search of the area will be conducted. Normal Republicans in the area will be alerted. Staff will possibly think about commencing to consider the possibility of starting the process of beginning to activate the community alerting system. Whatever it is. Neighborhoods where an e-mail list-serve exists will never know, as they are paid to look at LL Bean or porn all day. If another Democrat is located, after weighing all the factors, staff will take the action that is in the best interest of the safety of the community. The Police Department will always put the safety of normal Republican homes and luxury vehicles first.

In the Bitterroot

Selling Pop

I always thought my Dad must have dropped like a pine cone into the forest. Or that he was discovered by his mother and father, formed of leaves and twigs, as if made by Andy Goldsworthy, on a high meadow after a spring thaw. One summer in the 1930s he sat in a clearing in the woods, within a wooden booth his father had helped him to build. The booth was full of bottles of root beer. It had taken a long time, with his father's charming, natural deliberation, several trips around the logging camp, and into town, to look for scrap lumber and hardware, the way he slowly measured and marked a thing, twice, three times. Carpentry wasn't my grandfather's forte, but it was his refuge; he hibernated in it.

The woods and the stuff of men: the flaking sides of the lumberjacks' bunkhouses, the electric lights strung in the trees violated little or nothing, were as much a part of the woods as the brushes of pine needles around Dad's feet, the knot holes which grimaced on the trees outside his bedroom window, the high-altitude silence of noon.

All around Dad was in casual order. A truck rusted quietly near the machine shop, listening to the chirps and drillings, rushes and peckings of the summer woods, although it still had a few corroded parts to offer. Here and there, piles of things which men and boys might put to use slept, seductive: half-done spools of wire, slats, black enamel door knobs, hinges, saw horses, several moods of the wheel. Dad knew these stores thoroughly and while he sat in his box of junior commerce his mind roved over them, testing, selecting, combining, imagining what might be done with each and every thing.

In his bedroom there was a shelf, carpentered by his father, next to his bed, on which were four blankets and a thick comforter of worn, olive-green sateen. In winter Dad often woke to find his bed covered with drifting snow, although he was perfectly warm down in the deep heart of the bed. On the shelf, three thick volumes of *The Boy Mechanic*, books so full of things, dreams and hope it seemed infinite. How many times had he told himself that he was going to glance through the whole of one volume of it before going to sleep? – only to wake in the morning, his nose inserted at page 35, Build Your Own Indian Canoe? Half the projects in *The Boy Mechanic* were to be made from helmets left over from the First World War. There weren't a lot of them kicking around the Bitterroot Valley, though once a pal had found nine of them in his uncle's wood shed. He handed them out among his friends and that Christmas in the camp there were gifts of helmet reading lamps, ashtrays and floral vases. An Inexpensive and Functional Chick Incubator May Be Made From

Standard Soldiers' Helmets. Even if the Indian Canoe was one of the fancier wonders in *The Boy Mechanic*, and you would have to buy lumber to make it, the great resource needed to make your canoe, reading lamp, smoker's cabinet, camp kitchen or working electric trolley was around them all: time.

Dad dreamt, on weekends and holidays, of the bourgeoning, mundane materials all around him in the green high-altitude world. Paraffin, tin, blotting paper, kerosene, packing crates, railroad spikes, milk pails and, of paramount use, wooden kegs and barrels. Egg Beater Made Into Winder For Model Airplanes, Shield For Heater In Chick Brooding House, Cheese-Grate And Ash Tray Made From A Tin Can, A Small Working Pile Driver, Squirrel-Skin Bill Fold. Blotter Attached To Wrist Saves Time.

His Pop

was Superintendent of the logging camp. He always wore a Mackinaw, being from Michigan. *Writes checks and wears them*, the lumberjacks said of him. When Dad was young my grandfather was very large and moved slowly through the snow or the summer grass. Because of his girth he constructed a unique desk for himself in the office he shared with his colleague MacKenzie – what else would be the name of a man sharing a stove-heated office, fir trees out the window?

In later years my grandfather's wintered nose and slow gestures made him seem an Indian. When describing life in the Bitterroot his eyes and hands traced the horizons of it cannily, austerely.

At five in the morning my grandfather walked from the family's little frame house across the camp to the office cabin, already thinking about his desk, how he would arrange it, about the ledger sheets he would work on during the day. He opened the door and turned on the dim bulb. He loaded the stove with thick bark and lit it. He raised the dark green window shade, for he liked to watch it grow light as he worked the first few hours at his desk, liked to watch the men rise and go painfully to the cook house for their breakfast, then emerging with a few jokes and a little talk, kidding each other on the way to the latrine.

The desk was made from a previous desk, an indifferent one, with a knee hole and drawers on either side, but my grandfather had fixed to this an enormous, moveable top, of thick boards bound together and covered with red linoleum. It could be raised to an angle, like a draughtsman's table. It was a joy to my grandfather that there were many things he could put on the surface of his desk which wouldn't slide off, even if it were steeply inclined. His metal ash tray and packet of Lucky Strikes, the heavy Bakelite telephone. The more work he had to do and the harder he wished to concentrate, the more steeply he set his desk top.

Coming in half an hour after my grandfather, MacKenzie could tell what sort of a day it was to be by the angle of the desk. If it were nearly vertical, the ashtray and Luckies perched at the upper edge, this was very bad. A winter angle, a tell-tale gnomon of hard work and fierce company loyalty. Some men in the camp knew my grandfather only as a hat and the rims of spectacles seen over the edge of the desk. On the other hand there were spring days, and days in early fall, when everything breathed that it had been taken care of, and MacKenzie would come in to find the desk nearly level (a slight angle still signifying precise overseeing), my grandfather with his feet up on it, smiling and smoking with the enamel mug of pig-awful coffee he'd heated on the stove.

At the upper left-hand corner of the desk, tucked under the metal strip which bound the edge of it, was a picture of my grandfather and grandmother at Glacier, a time he remembered as white – white light under the canvas, her hair at last undone, the lacing and unlacing of their boots, which became a game; coffee and bacon, the triangle of the beautiful West seen through the end of the tent . . .

When he had pitched his desk appropriately to the season and his sense of obligations, he got out his fountain pen, mechanical pencil and red lead pencil. His job was to observe, budget, requisition, account, report. A supply sergeant in the war in France, these were the tools he had been given, along with accountancy paper, and he used these alone for the rest of his life: the fountain pen's knowledge and delineating confidence, the pencil's calculating caginess, the wary warnings of red lead.

I have a few of his writing tools. My neurotic appetite for pens and pencils swells my collection shamefully beyond his three-item system of genius, but I organise my life on paper as he did on his giant desk. Was Dad chagrined by this ascetic aesthetic? Did he feel strictured as a boy by black, blue-black and red? He has never shown me a favourite writing instrument. He makes a point of picking up whatever pen or pencil is at hand, blinking at it with an expression of surprise, before going to work on his ream of pointedly plain white paper.

– Jonsson's cut his finger off, said MacKenzie, stepping into the office. Clean off. My grandfather rotated slowly towards MacKenzie in his chair, already picturing Jonsson's finger on his desk, an element of The Report on the red plain of control. – Ha ha! He turned to his desk, sharply raised it, and wrote on a company memorandum blank with the fountain pen. He calculated the costs to the labour pool and to the supply room with his pencil, and made a sign, NO HOT LUNCH. COOK INJURED, with the red lead pencil.

Abdul the . . .

The family bundled themselves into town, into a house with real heating, so that my Dad could go to high school without having to ski to it or get lost in the snow. He and his friend George hung around together. George was tall and had a sophisticated overcoat he had got in Colorado Springs. On cold days they liked to walk around downtown, looking with satisfaction at the snow mounded on the low commercial buildings, the radio store, the butcher's. They would go into the music shop and listen to a few records, see if there were any girls doing the same. Dad always had his trumpet with him, hoping to get tips on playing it. George

scoffed at this but Dad was persistent. Someone had seen Fred
Waring in town a few months back, buying tyre chains and liquor.

– Here, said George, what are you going to do next year? Walk
around town with that thing? I'm going to college in California
to study science. The Navy's going to put me through. Why don't
you come along? Dad had been putting off thinking about what
would happen after graduation. He didn't want to choose. He
liked the space and the quiet and the way things were organised.
Trees. A little music on Saturdays. But he would never get this
peace and quiet again whatever he did. – OK. – Have you seen the
new juke boxes? slurped George. He had acquired a pipe to go with
his overcoat. His self-promoted air of being college bound. They
walked more quickly now on the slippery sidewalks. They had not
seen any girls and George was determined on whatever excitement
could be squeezed out of their town on a winter Friday.

Someone had had *this* idea: instead of filling a lot of juke boxes
with records, you have one collection of records at a central location
and play them down a telephone line to small boxes around town,
as requested. Whoever had had this entertainment brainstorm
couldn't interest many merchants in having a box, so most of these
were located out of doors, where people did *not* tend to congregate
for entertainment. There was one at the filling station. – Got a
nickel? said George. – What are we hearing? said Dad. – *Hello,
music lovers. What is your Hit Parade Request?* said the box in the
voice of an attractive girl. – Abdul the Bulbul Ameer, said George.
– *What!* – Abdul the Bulbul Ameer. – *What is THAT?* – It's a
song. – *I never heard of it.* – What do you mean? said George,

it's funny. It's on the air all the time. I just heard it last night. – Me too, said Dad. – *Who are you?* – I'm his friend. – *Only one customer per coin.* – It's my dime, said Dad. – *Well, how do you spell it?* George leaned way over, close to the cloth-covered microphone. – A-B-D-U-L. – *Then what?* – Oh come on, said George. Either you've got it or you haven't. Everyone's humming it. Do you know how cold it is out here? – *Oh,* said the box, in a pretty fluster, *I think I – how does it go again?* George looked at Dad and shook his head. He took his pipe out of his mouth and grasped the sides of the box, to get its full attention. – 'The sons of the Prophet are hardy and bold . . . ' – *Keep going.* He sang the whole thing, Ivan Skavinsky Skivar, the maiden, the fountain, the Danube. It was currently his favourite song. That was why he had requested it. – *Thanks,* said the box, and went dead. – What about my dime? said George. The thing remained silent. – My dime, said Dad. – Where's its office? George demanded. – I think it's in the Eagle Hotel. They looked at each other, George in his overcoat, Dad with his trumpet case and earflap hat. They went up the icy street.

Trout Farm

Dad would take me along on his errands. When they were done, we often found ourselves tooling around in county land, a collection of odd ditches, egg farms, stands of mummified eucalyptus. There were *attractions* hidden out here – little old amusements I thought of as radiating out from Disneyland, connected to it by a kind of electricity. If I had the good fortune to recognise a dirt road hidden by a certain stand of eucalyptus, I could say *the trout farm*, let's go to the trout farm. And Dad would generally turn the Brown Car there; he liked it. I think sometimes he'd planned we'd go there but not tell me: he derived pleasure from suddenly presenting a thing to you. We all labour in secret.

If he'd told me we were going to the trout farm when we got into the car, he'd have heard about nothing but the trout farm for two hours, my ridiculous theories about it, while he bought gas, went to the hardware store and the nursery. The errands of men together. I would plan on which rowboat to get and would worry that we wouldn't get the dark green one that had dark green oars.

What the hell are you worried about? I thought you liked the trout farm. I do. *You're not going to regurgitate are you?* I was worried that this time wouldn't be *exactly* like last time. I depended on things I loved to be always the same.

We drove into the eucalyptus and went this way and that: they'd made the road meander, like a *ride*, because they were from the Midwest and had Midwestern ideas of how to really pull in the folks. We came into the open and parked by a red shack, which looked like a general store or bait shop beside a Missouri river. There was a thermometer advertising something, a porch, a cooler of pop. Behind the shack was a miniature dock where a few flaking rowboats rode the glaucous water of the pond, which was lined with cement. Once when we were sitting in our dark green boat I asked Dad how deep the pond was. He looked down at the drab water and snorted, *about four feet if I don't miss my guess.* Possibly I'd interrupted his musings.

Dad got out of the car and shut the door. He put his hands in his pockets and squinted and looked around, casually. This is how you show the kind of people who run trout farms you're just like them. Which can save you a lot of money, he said. He was wearing the old trousers from a brown suit. So he'd known we were going to come to the trout farm. He walked slowly across the deep gravel to the shack, where an old guy in the *echt* battered grey cap slid back a window. So everything was repeating itself just fine. Because they both came from some world vanished out of here, they bantered. Because I was born in southern California, I could not understand slow transactions. The old fellow said

82

things to me that were like ruffling my hair; old guys from places outside California could do that without touching you.

We walked out on the dock and looked down at the rowboats, which were fugitives from a forgotten city park. *This here's a good one*, said the old guy, still *doing* the old guy. They were all the same, but they were not all dark green. *We need that one*, I said. (Did you hear me? We *need* it, I whispered to Dad.) *He wants those green oars*, he said to the old guy. The old guy looked at me and handed us my favourites, the most important dark green oars.

Something silly about casting off, waving goodbye from a three-foot dock in a concrete pond no deeper than a bath and no wider than a grocery store. Or is there? Dad put the oars in the locks and began to row us around, and to muse. *You know, if you were going to get picky*, he said, *I wouldn't have wasted my energy on all that goddamn banter.* Ease was the most important delicacy in dealing with these people.

We rowed to the middle of the pond. That didn't take long. This was the only body of water I had ever been on. I wondered if this did anything at all for Dad or if he just wanted to eat fish – when he dipped the green oars in the water, was he thinking of the lakes of the north where he'd had real solitude, where there was scenery that had not been swept aside? Or manufactured, for that matter. *Got your pole?* He attached a sinker and a red and white float to my line. I liked this float and had taken it into my bath. Now it was going to get dirty. I took the hook in my hand and put a squishy piece of bait on it. *We're all set!* His cantillation.

We dropped our lines over the gunwale and waited about ten seconds. A strong fish started yanking frantically on the line, out of boredom. These fish lived in close quarters. According to Mom, they were hysterical. We tried to make this as exciting as we could, given that the trout insisted on being caught. *OK. OK. Reel him in.*

I got him! We took pity on the most bored-looking one and put him into the smelly creel. Dad caught one and then I caught another. They flopped around in the creel for a long time. They were strong from eating their own poo. The way the old guy explained it to us, he scooped the trout poo up off the bottom of the pond once a month and put it in a hand-cranked machine which made pellets of it, which he gave you for bait. *Haven't put any real food in there for twelve years*, he said. *I think they're being short-changed*, said Dad. *Not in there long enough to matter.*

While we were there a tank truck pulled in and delivered more trout. A man just opened a cock on the end of the truck and a rush that was half fish and half water thundered out. He spat in the pond and drove off. *Time to head for shore, mate*, said Dad. The oars glistened with stuff more solid than liquid so I guessed he was right about the depth. It was hot. It was time for our reward.

The old guy took the creel and weighed our fish. *Three big ones, huh? You want 'em cleaned?* Dad paid him and he went out back to gut them and wrap them in the *News Tribune*. Dad looked over at the soda cooler and down at me. *Probably time for some refreshment, mate. No grape for you, though.* I picked out my usual bottle of Nesbitt's orange and we sat on the porch. Out back the old guy was flipping the fish guts straight into the pond. It really was hot. I started to think about the shallow pond, full of poos, the spit, the guts. The Nesbitt's was none too cold. *Here you are, folks, all wrapped up!*

Blugggh!

Hey!

That guy was pretty surprised, said Dad. *At least you threw up in the pond and not in the cooler.*

When we got home Mom exhibited her querulous attitude towards food that did not come from the supermarket. *Whaddya think they raise 'em for?* growled Dad. *They're not tropical fish for looking at. I'll have to make a hamburger for your son*, she said. *And what*, he said, turning on me, *is the matter with eating the fish you caught? That is the goddamndest thing. Do you realise that I ate a fish I caught myself every day of my life when I was your age? And in winter I sawed through the ice to get them.* He stamped outside to wash his hands under the garden hose, a sign that he was really vexed; when faucets were too fancy a thing. It was true that I hated fish. I only liked being with him.

Unis

Occasionally They would try to whip up a kind of empty enthusiasm for something we were supposed to enjoy, something we were meant to ALREADY KNOW was 'enjoyable'. Was 'fun'. It really bothered me, all the stuff you were ALREADY supposed to know. This jerk-off gym teacher who tried to teach me how to drive, in high school, was astonished I'd never driven a car before. How the Hell was I supposed to have done that? The *look* he gave me said it all: your father is a ball-less, law-abiding FRUIT. Everyone cheats in America. Don't you KNOW that? Later the same guy approached me in the library and *sized me up*. He told me I ought to join the Wrestling Team. He squeezed my upper arm and shoulder and I punched him in the mouth.

The circus was one of these things we knew we ought to be Excited About. In the car, Dad said to Mom, This is 1960, dear, don't you think the circus is possibly your elephant? What he meant was irrelevant. It was your elephant because we were already suspicious of anything that wasn't on television. I was totally brainwashed by television *and* school, and my sister was being brainwashed by me. I had aversions: to leaving the house, certainly an aversion to DISCOMFORT of any kind involving getting up early, getting home late, driving too far, sitting outdoors, SMELLING ANIMALS, getting dirty or, especially, dusty, so on. I particularly hated going *all the way to Los Angeles* for almost anything.

But while They didn't really think the circus was OK (tawdry, sick), it turned out *we* thought it was OK, although we were freaked out by the weird food. I had thought it would be like the movies, whereas the main thing seemed to be *hot peanuts in a bag*. The only popcorn came coloured pink, the kernels fused together into a heavy, stale BLOCK. What's with this popcorn? I asked. It's easier to transport from town to town of course, said my Dad, who cares about the popcorn, why don't you pay attention to what's going ON down there?

This was the proverbial 'three-ring circus', the combined efforts of the Ringling Brothers, Barnum and Bailey. They had to come up with this to compete with the cinema and television. It was hard to know where to look. My sister kept crying when she thought she'd missed something. There seemed to be endless processions, girls in feathered headdresses on elephants, etc. While we were just *sitting* there, my Mom's whole childhood was being destroyed, it seemed, eaten away in front of her eyes! She thought the whole thing had turned into Vegas stuff. Well, maybe it had – obviously they'd had to do *something* to STAY IN BUSINESS.

My sister liked the animals, whereas animals bored me rigid. I was already too brainwashed to dig an actual tiger. I was unimpressed with the *quality of the clowning* (a phrase I picked up somewhere which has proved useful in political thinking), except when they slap-boxed each other with enormous, cartoon-like flat gloves. I needed a pair of these immediately, I thought. Because of SCHOOL.

My Uncle Reginald was sitting to my left and he kept getting up and making his way across us all and down the grandstand, time and again, first to buy himself a beer (he was bored by children and who isn't?), then to relieve himself and also buy a beer. During the few minutes he was actually in his seat, he became incensed with the people in front of *him*, who were also a restless bunch, getting up, putting coats on and off, waving souvenir pennants about. Reginald decided he'd missed some feeble manoeuvre by a drugged ocelot way off in the far ring and went nuts: IF YOU'DA SAT DOWN, WE'DA SEEN THE SHOW!

He seemed to want to perpetuate the age-old drink/circus incompatibility. The *fired clowns* beloved of Hollywood. But there is something sad and awful about circuses – all this FAKE FUN causes psychosis. So as usual Reginald had to be shushed by my Aunt Edith, dragged down and then taken out. My sister also had to be taken out, near the end, when they were going to shoot this guy out of a cannon. She started screaming immediately they drove this thing into the ring, just like Uncle Reginald.

But a few acts before the cannon was *the* amazing act that defined both the circus and the family: UNIS. Unis was a dapper guy in top hat, tails and white gloves. He came out with the usual 'lovely assistant' and did a few dumb-looking stunts, twirling a hoop on one leg; god I thought, I can do that. But then things got a little more interesting. Unis suddenly sprang back, turned himself upside down, and started walking around the ring on his hands, twirling his hoops on his ankles. THEN he started hopping around on ONE hand, adding a hoop to his free hand. *Great.* Then still twirling everything he went up and down a ladder on one hand. My sister and I were transfixed. I don't know why this impressed me so, but it did. Maybe because he looked like a nice guy, a *reasonable* guy, and I was always for any imposed normality being turned on its head. It occurred to me that he ought to have put wires in his tail-coat so that he would look *less* upside down, in the same way that when I imagined walking on the ceiling of my room the blood wouldn't rush to my head or my pyjamas flap up over my stomach. But for the *pièce de résistance*: the lovely assistant wheeled out a large illuminated GLASS BALL. Unis hopped over to it. He managed to get up on the glass ball as they narrowed and narrowed the spotlight and all the your elephant stuff came to a halt. And THEN he slowly closed his hand, finger by finger, until he was standing upside down on top of the glass ball on *one white-gloved finger*. I drooled on to my popcorn block. Ta-daaa!

In the course of three hours my mother had gone totally sceptical of the circus. In the parking lot she told me it was impossible, nobody could stand on one finger, he must have had some kind of brace for his finger and arm. You *saw* it, I said. Why was he wearing gloves, that's what I want to know, she said. No no, that's what makes it great, I said, the gloves make it slippery, so it's harder.

There was a fearsome amount of real junk for sale in the circus parking lot, this was another reason it was an uncomfortable place to visit. My father and sister were trapped between two cars by a seedy-looking soul who had a load of battery-operated electric cats. Rather my father was trapped between this guy AND MY SISTER.

What made Unis an important moment in the family's life: the next day was Monday and first thing that morning my mother phoned up and *made an appointment with the doctor.* What seems to be the matter, asked the nurse. Nothing, nothing, I just need to see him, my mother said. So she got in there and astonished the doctor by telling him all about the circus and how it had declined probably, and was SMUT now, and then leaned closer to him, holding her bag, and told him about Unis's act. And what I wanted to see you about, she said, was it's not possible, is it? You can't stand on one finger! The doctor looked out the window for a minute and said, of course it's possible. It's a BONE, isn't it? Is *that* what you came in here for? I was waiting in the car and she did tell me honestly what happened, but still refused to believe it.

He was wearing gloves, she yelled at the dinner table. *He must have had a stiffener.* I'll bet he didn't have as many as Reginald, my father mumbled. All these *schisms* as regarded belief SHIMMERED through the life of the family. If she wasn't going to believe in UNIS, who was knocking his brains out to stand on one finger right in front of her, then *I* sure as hell was not going along with this JESUS baloney.

The Better Burger Bureau

Being small for your age, it is many years before you are able to see out of the window of the Family Car. Father is fond of driving; by the time you are ten or eleven you have travelled over 100,000 miles on various holidays. You have been a first-hand witness to motel signs, gasoline pumps, and a ton o' sky. Pardner.

There is little to think about, there in the back seat, except about what you are going to eat next. This is primitive; savage. Your sister wraps her head in a blanket, crossing the Mojave Desert, and whimpers – she's buried so deep no one knows if it's boredom or the ferocious heat.

At this time, for reasons you cannot divine, you are allowed to eat many hamburgers. Your parents weren't the types to allow previously this kind of monaural diet: almost every meal you eat is 'balanced', in the US Department of Agriculture sense, to the point of absurdity. Not that parents ever listen to anything you say, but you did tell them one day that a hamburger contained all the proper elements of nutrition (as it was then understood): starch, protein, 'roughage', certain necessary fats . . . (Given the diktats of the age, this wasn't so insane.) Sometimes your parents simply *tired* of imposing their excessive, 1950s-induced vigilant paranoia and just let you *have* something.

Is there a Commie in that ketchup?

Growing up in America, you have always known there is PLENTY. You might not have access always to the *totality* of plenty, if you are poor, or if you are an over-regulated ten-year-old, but always, always, you have known it is there, the plenty, the surfeit – and there were always ways to get it. *DEMAND* it, or *make some money*: the idea that *that* is always possible.

Hamburger Deluxe

is what you want: it is what you must have in America. Forget your health and forget history – but forget too the fast-food chains, and get you to a really crappy-looking diner or a smelly coffee shop, the kind where they keep wiping the tables with this suspiciously grey lump of flannel that makes your mother scream and her hair stand on end. Hamburger deluxe, in its classical period (c. 1945–1965) was this: an OVAL PLATTER (very important) on which rests the actual hamburger itself, which ought to be on a sesame-seed bun (given the flaccidity of American bread, these little *helping seeds* stiffen it and give it flavour). The cooking degree of choice is MEDIUM (the enjoyment of rare meat is *thousands of years in the future*). Everything in America is, at this time, MEDIUM – your hamburger, your shirt, your thoughts. The bun may be lightly toasted; the top should be left to one side, face up – this is your invitation to GARNISH the hamburger deluxe, with the very materials which *make* it 'deluxe': also on the oval platter will be a leaf of lettuce, two slices of sweet butter pickle or a small GHERKIN, and a tiny paper cup of dressing, and one of cole slaw. These must have been very valuable. The dressing is sometimes warm mayonnaise, turning clear, but more usually 'Russian' dressing, an obtuse combination of ketchup and mayonnaise – one hesitates to speculate what is supposed to be 'Russian' about it, except that it's crap – remember this is 1960, you're being taken back in time for your hamburger deluxe. On you go. Ketchup is in a squeezy bottle at your table, your BOOTH. Mustard is anathema. One hears it is taken in the East. There will not be any French fries included with your hamburger deluxe – this happens later – more usual would be a tiny paper packet containing two or three potato crisps from a distant industrial city.

You know there is PLENTY; you also have the youthful American feeling everything is IMPROVING. All signs tell you so. The plenty of America is constantly multiplying *and* being improved: BETTER plenty. It is also being made more interesting; friendlier . . . One of the ways you find this out, glean some small experience from your holiday in the back seat, is to acquire and read BROCHURES. Thousands of these are available at every gas station and in each motel lobby.

How else are you to know that the WONDER STUMP is only 300 miles ahead? Or that individual concrete teepees offer hot and cold running water, pay TV, and air conditioning? What your parents have to put up with, besides the thousands of miles of driving and the intense heat, is a frightening barrage of information from the back seat about caverns, model villages and other 'authentic' side-trip experiences they can't possibly give a turd about, let alone afford, either in terms of time or money. You must also commandeer the Family's motel guide, that of the American Automobile Association, the 'Triple A'. From this, drone out long lists of the attributes of motels in the half-dead town where the Family will no doubt spend the night, or the town you passed seventy-five miles back where you *should* have spent the night. Pool, air conditioning, TV, no TV, pay TV, fireplace, kitchenettes . . . It couldn't possibly have made any difference. All you and your sister want is a splash in the pool, hamburger deluxe, and to see something, *anything* on TV, since you have seen nothing all day except the backs of your parents' heads.

But peruse this AAA guide book, almost GOVERN-MENTAL in its strict and impartial evaluations. (Indeed, the AAA is *still* reminiscent of a little government – visit one of its offices – there is an atmosphere of utilitarian steel chairs and furtive lunches taken from vending machines, unique in this age – the offices of the telephone company used to look and smell like this until 'it' realised it could rip people off like crazy and wallow in executive luxuries.) But you find there is something going on: EVALUATION. CRITICISM. And nothing suits you better, the little king of the back seat, Lord of the Info.

There are a few overly canny recommendations in this book about where to eat in most of the half-dead towns, although as a Family you are for the most part happy to find the hamburger deluxe. 'And a salad'. But you have also discovered the existence of *Duncan Hines*. He is a white-haired portly chap who has apparently, somehow, eaten in every restaurant in the United States. Occasionally he advertises things on TV, where he sort of flubbers about like Alfred Hitchcock. He also gives his name to cake mixes, in boxes. But here is another CRITIC. With people prepared to criticise the motel you are staying in and the food you are given, things are bound to get better and better, aren't they? Don't you see a career opportunity here? If you got *paid* for *complaining*, they couldn't hold it against you in the front seat, could they?

Besides, the plenty, the plenty is constantly *improving itself.* You put two and two together, and taking the logotype of the AAA for your own, you create the Better Burger Bureau. You create it by buying an orange notebook at a gas station and drawing BBB on it.

Voilà! Now you search out hamburgers and tear into them with the zeal of a frightened, middle-achieving academic. You will not agree to visit any restaurant which does not offer hamburger deluxes. You pull out your BBB notebook as a knife from its sheath, luncheon and dinner. You SNEER while your sister orders peanut butter and jelly, your mother, your *own mother* a salad, your father all kinds of ridiculous food you never heard of and which he only orders on holiday: pot roasts, patty melts, BLTs, Reuben sandwiches . . .! Whereas you, YOU will soon know all there is to be known about all the hamburger deluxes in the west. You *fools*.

Think you're doing quite well, *rating* everything from the oval platter to the bun to the butter pickles. Until you get to *Red's Café*.

Can't say where it is, could be anywhere of course, but it is plumb in the middle of this your vacation. You are all very tired. Today has been one of your father's 600-mile days, days on which he gets everyone up at six in the morning, forcibly stuffs you with cold cereal and bundles you into the car before digestion has even begun, even before the manager of the motel is awake, which always *fills you with fear*. Fear of *perceived abscondment*. You are all gasping for your usual day-end refreshments. Why are not moderate amounts of beer available to children who have been sat in the back of a car in the desert all day? A six-pack each would do.

The motel pool, despite the Triple A, is nonexistent or minimal or suggestive of disease, so *back into the car*, to find somewhere to eat. *Red's* is it around here. At first everything seems to suggest, to *boast*, the requisites of the hamburger deluxe – icky rag, uncomfortable seating, a waitress that makes your mother's hair stand on end. Take out your all-important orange notebook, man of the world, a cake-franchiser, a motel-stayer after all. But you are *not prepared* for the first truly bad hamburger deluxe of your life, your *career*, after all. You taste this, this *thing*, which seems to have been cooked in fish grease (there were no edible fish in western America until 1980), and burst into tears – grieving for the thousands of miles between Red's and the safe hamburger deluxes of home, weary with the endless, fryingly hot vacation where nothing is seen. The bun is half stale and half soggy, the meat revolting, the Russian dressing tastes like what it is, vomit. This hamburger deluxe is threatening to topple your whole system. The BBB has taken a tremendous right hook and staggers . . .

Blugggh!

Hey!

Of course you savage Red's in the strict AAA-like columns of the BBB. From the back seat, you read out your review on subsequent days until the plashing, familial laughter turns to quiet bemusement, then brooding reflection. But you are no Duncan Hines, you will never be able to eat this many hamburgers. You have beheld the disturbing, dangling underbelly of the dream.

Now, of course, such hamburger hesitancy is unthinkable – this dish has brought a once-proud nation to its knees. And you are not supposed to criticise anything in the United States anyway.

Imagine Thoreau encountering a hamburger deluxe. He would find much to criticise, of course, but the easy availability, the comradely qualities of these pioneer meals might mean he would no longer need to steal fruit from the Emersons. And Georgie Babbitt, ahh – he would relish them like nothing else.

Thoreau

And yet he rated it as a gain, coming to America, that here you could get tea, and coffee, and meat every day. But the only true America is that country where you are at liberty to pursue such a mode of life as may enable you to do without these, and where the state does not endeavor to compel you to sustain the slavery and war and other superfluous expenses which directly or indirectly result from the use of such things.

Walden

Even as Thoreau sought to remind his countrymen, 'Americans', of what he saw as their *essential* freedoms, they were slipping away. What would he have made of the introduction of the income tax? Of the permanent arms economy? Hell, what would he have made of *CNN*?

I am sure that I never read any memorable news in a newspaper. If we read of one man robbed, or murdered, or killed by accident, or one house burned, or one vessel wrecked, or one steamboat blown up, or one cow run over on the Western Railroad, or one mad dog killed, or one lot of grasshoppers in the winter, – we never need read of another. One is enough. If you are acquainted with the principle, what do you care for a myriad instances and applications?

The speed and emptiness of the coming American life appalled him: 'It lives too fast,' he said of my country 150 years ago. As some have pointed out, Thoreau would have had us all eating out of his hand if it were not for his occasional eruptions of egomania, and what in America is called 'bitterness', which in Europe means 'realism'. But his works other than *Walden* are full of a mordant, exquisitely-observed humour, the comedy of human behaviour. *A Week on the Concord and Merrimack Rivers* and *Cape Cod* are deeply felt, moving, fascinating books of a unique, philosophical slant; you could wish he had brought more of their good humour to *Walden* – it might indeed have been the book he wanted, heard round the world, instead of, now, feebly chirping in a few high schools.

It's easy to characterise him as a crank, of course, which is what numbskulls love to do – wandering around in his old clothes, that weird *neck beard*, stealing fruit from Emerson's dining-room table, screaming about the evil of coffee. He has always been treated as a crank in England. Perhaps it is because of his dedicated Brit-bashing: 'as for England, almost the last significant scrap of news from that quarter was the revolution of 1649.' But English people don't like Thoreau's kind of talk because they never came up with a way of dealing with the Industrial Revolution themselves, of humanising it; can't conceive of standing up to its implications and miseries even now. And they realise that today they only do American things, in that half-assed British way, so they don't like to hear these things criticised. 'The government of the world I live in was not framed, like that of Britain, in after-dinner conversation over the wine.' He was nothing if not a true democrat, one of the most vociferous of world citizens.

He talked a little too much about Indians, of both varieties, to make his contemporaries very comfortable. In *Walden* he harasses his Americans with much wisdom from the Vedas, and with the often more sensitive, righteous ways of living of the indigenous peoples. He had formed a large project in his mind about the native Americans, and travelled west to investigate the condition of their physical and political life. After spending time in Thoreau's America you begin to wonder if this, too, mightn't have been a book that would have changed history. Tuberculosis put paid to that.

Thoreau had excellent questions for every one of us, questions that become more pointed, more urgent with every passing year. *What are men celebrating?* What is the true value of a man's labour, of his life? And why do we need ALL THIS STUFF? 'It appears as if men had deliberately chosen the common mode of living because they preferred it to any other. Yet they honestly believe there is no choice left.'

There are some problems with the writing of *Walden* which

show discrepancies in Thoreau which he would never have wanted displayed – he was desperate to be a whole man and was afraid of seeming a false prophet, though he wasn't. Once in a while you get the sense of what trying to put up with his persistent optimism must have been like – a lot of people couldn't take it. 'Many a forenoon have I stolen away, preferring to spend thus the most valued part of the day; for I was rich, if not in money, in summer hours and summer days, and spent them lavishly' – Elwood P Dowd speaking.

He was, no doubt, a Christian of a sort, though it doesn't seem to have wrecked his thinking. His treatment of scripture and religious practice as a sort of friendly backdrop to his own arguments must have seemed blasphemous to some – it wouldn't have made him over many friends among the hoity-toity of Concord. He seems to have decided that the gospels, fortunately for them, and he were more or less in agreement, that they were speaking more or less the same language (he can rant like Jerry Falwell, though of course in a noble cause). He wasted a bit of time in wanting clerics to be intelligent and churches to be charitable, despite his urgings towards self-sufficiency. He just doesn't bother with the intricacies of something you might think he'd have had *infinite* squabbles with: he was happy enough to have a 'heavenly father', and to take charge of things from the next rung down.

OR, he doesn't believe in any of it and uses the religious context only as a way of communicating with us idiots.

Speaking of us, we tried his patience any number of times:

'I confess I do not make any very broad distinction between the illiterateness of my townsman who cannot read at all and the illiterateness of him who had learned to read what is only for children and feeble intellects.' Fortunate too that he is not alive to hear about Harry Potter.

One of the larger chinks in *Walden*, larger than the holes he describes in the house he built himself, which let in dandy draughts for the fireplace, is his grappling with the question of the individual v. the state. He never quite worked it out, though *Walden* was his most concentrated go at it. 'To act collectively is in the spirit of our institutions,' he says, but, elsewhere, 'if I knew for certainty that a man was coming to my house with the conscious design of doing me good, I should run for my life.' At such moments, all right, he leans on a fence rail, chewing a piece of grass, the greatest *kibitzer* of the nineteenth century. You can get the feeling he addicted himself to the idea of a goal for humanity he wasn't *quite* sure of, that he stood up time and again like a poor soul in an AA meeting who won't, who *can't* shut up.

In going to live in the woods, Thoreau had two things in mind – first to reduce life to its essentials, an aesthetic and ascetic experience, one you suppose was for its own sake. (He had a gloating interest in the masochistic practices of foreign mystics.) His second object was an economic experiment, to see what a person could make for himself and thereby reduce his dependence on the more insidious aspects of society and the economy. Far from turning his back on civilisation, he simply, and neatly, tried to step aside from it for two years. Far from renouncing intercourse with the world, he wanted to see if the things that hold us in thrall and apart from each other could be purified, or even eliminated. So – a Proudhon or a Bartleby? A bit of both. America had to be remade, even started all over again, he thought, and he was writing *Walden* only seventy-one years after the republic came into being. The stink of business was already bothering him – 'trade curses everything it handles'. (It seems sad that he died before the Civil War had reached its resolution – the struggle for abolition suited Thoreau's moral and rhetorical talents admirably, and he contributed to it with passion, as a staunch defender of Captain John Brown, and helping escaped slaves travelling through Massachusetts on the underground railroad.) That this re-examination of our obligations to each other, and our desires, makes *Walden* one of the most thoughtful, *stillest* books about man and nature.

People, *men* if you have to give them a name, have always got fed up with their encumbrances and given them up, tried to run away – the ones that never come back get called priests. In 1212, Kamo no Chomei got fed up with his life and stuff in Japan. Through his spiritual studies he 'became aware of the meaning of things', which sounds very like 'awakening', a word which runs straight through *Walden*. Kamo wrote in a beautiful short treatise, 'An Account of My Hut': 'before I became aware, I had become heavy with years, and with each remove my dwelling grew smaller.' He erects a small, one-room shelter, using a method similar to Thoreau's. 'I have built a little shelf on which I keep three or four black leather baskets that contain books of poetry and music and extracts from the sacred writings. Beside them stand a folding koto and a lute.' 'The view has no owner,' he tells us – 'only in a hut built for the moment can one live without fears.' Thinking on his efforts to survive alone, Kamo considers it is a sin to cause physical or mental pain: 'how can we borrow the labour of others?' There is a passage in *Walden* where Thoreau considers, favourably, as a dwelling, a large wooden box used for tools by men building the railway. It is little more than a coffin, though this doesn't seem to have struck him – going a little overboard here on the self-abnegation maybe. Kamo, though, is very satisfied with his last, box-like dwelling: 'A bare two carts would suffice to carry off the whole house, and except for the carter's fee there would be no expenses at all.' Which Thoreau himself could have written 600 years later, and with joy. (Their respective attitudes to encroaching snow, however, were rather different.)

Thoreau was hugely amused by the reactions of friends and the curious who came to inspect his household, whether he was there or not ('how came Mrs. — to know my sheets were not as clean as hers?'). Many seemed to feel he was in some sort of *danger*, only a few miles from civilisation, though he dismisses these: 'they would not go a-huckleberrying without a medicine chest'. He was amused, more than put out, by his lack of space: 'One inconvenience I sometimes experienced in so small a house, the difficulty of getting to a sufficient distance from my guest when we began to utter the big thoughts in big words. You want room for your thoughts to get into sailing trim and run a course or two before they make their port.' (This always reminds me of the equally scornful, equally exasperated Holden Caulfield in *The Catcher in the Rye*, when a guy his date knows at the theatre needs a lot of *room* to answer a simple question.)

What would the kindly ascetic, who would have cleansed us of the roots of some very bad American things, who went off meat and fish during his stay at the pond, make of the citizens of his country grown so corpulent that aeroplane seats, even ambulances have had to be re-engineered to accommodate them? 'The gross feeder is a man in the larva state; and there are whole nations in that condition, nations without fancy or imagination, whose vast abdomens betray them.'

Thoreau's *worry for us* is enduring and poignant. Thinking on the coming of the railway, he considered its whole impact on the environment, the lives of the men who laboured to construct it, and what it might bring to the American future, both good and bad: 'the railway is as broad as it is long'. (Even only in terms of the huge parcels of land the railroads snapped up, extending for miles beyond their necessary rights-of-way, he was right.)

Men have an indistinct notion that if they keep up this activity of joint stocks and spades long enough all will at length ride somewhere, in next to no time, and for nothing; but though a crowd rushes to the depot, and the conductor shouts 'All aboard!' when the smoke is blown away and the vapor condensed, it will be perceived that a few are riding, but the rest are run over, and it will be called, and will be, "A melancholy accident."

In those few lines there is much said on the roads to growth taken in America, much to chew on and to rue.

What is moving, *necessary*, about Thoreau is his foresight, his compassion, his obstinacy. He only wanted the best for us, hardly at all for himself. *Walden* is shot through with a nervous, cajoling optimism, made palatable and wonderful by his own failings, his unavoidable descents into an ironic, almost existential wit, something pretty thin on the ground in America today: 'Snipes and woodcocks may . . . afford rare sport, but I trust it would be nobler game to shoot one's self.' By which he meant to target yourself, make a trophy of your life; but I prize too the Beckettian *ombra* around that thought.

Thoreau never faltered.
EMERSON

Very Thoreau

Did my loathing for my classmates make me vulnerable to the genius of Thoreau, or in reading him did I have to come to abjure them and what they stood for? There is much in him of the unhappy adolescent, *for* the unhappy adolescent, and I ought to know.

It was his slow, almost maddeningly slow, description of leaves, of trees, that drew me in. Right away I recognised in Thoreau a fellow connoisseur of depression, if nothing else. Today, writing this, on the very Roof of Europe, I have three autumn leaves on my desk, and I'm working with an *italic pen*, just to annoy you!

Thoreau isn't straightforward – the *slipperiness* of his arguments causes some to think of him as a frantic, ill-considered soul. And there is nothing wrong with dipping into *Walden*, rather than sitting down with it . . . like taking a swim in Walden Pond itself: bracing and lovely. What a lot of people don't know. But I prefer to think that on a literary level he was a real master of ambiguity (though he was not quite a Mary Chase). He could have put his rhetorical talents to great bad, but he didn't: we are fortunate that Thoreau did not found the biggest advertising agency in America. With Freud at his side he might have been . . . gee whizz!

My banjo friend, K, and I were struck by what Thoreau *seemed* to be saying. And because I have never been able to fight free of the physical impresses of reading, I quickly made an idol of the family copy of Thoreau, covered in dark green cloth, a Viking Portable. I was back to my altar-making, for to my green Thoreau I added, for some kind of solace, a wooden recorder, an old dried-out chestnut my grand-uncle used to carry around with him, an Osmiroid italic fountain pen, and took to wearing a pair of brown hiking boots all the time (vestment). 'They who come rarely to the woods,' he wrote, 'take some little piece of the forest into their hands to play with by the way . . . '

I was disappointed to discover that Thoreau used to sit around playing the flute, as it's an instrument I've always disliked – it is incapable of expressing neurosis, what good is a musical instrument without a dark side? – and the flute repertoire includes the most saccharine, nauseating music ever written. However *Pete Seeger* used to noodle on the recorder a bit, so that was OK. My father's obsessive Nonesuch LP-collecting had steamrollered any interest I had in the Baroque, so I just played 'Living in the Country' like Pete. I would do this in our one available wilderness, a park in the hills above our town. Full of dust, really, and nondescript vegetation, and banana slugs you slipped on – yet once in a while you could glimpse what Thoreau was talking about.

The chestnut was something old Ohio men used to affect (the 'Buckeye State', after all) – keeping one in their pockets and polishing it with their fingers over the years, as you might a briar pipe. That I liked this small shiny thing, found some natural resonance in it, was pretty funny, considering that my grand-uncle was better known for falling asleep in his soup-plate than as a lover of nature. Golf was as close as he got, and given the cocktails involved in golf as he knew it, it was not very close.

The italic fountain pen gave whatever I wrote the instant authority of the older world, things written by candle light. What a jerk. But I still write with this kind of pen when I have something intimate or unpleasant to say. Hardly any kind of paper will take it any more.

The boots were all Seeger's fault too, as was my habit of wearing formal shirts and rolling the sleeves up. Desmond Morris once wrote that this is sexual provocation in human males – 'I'm stripping for action!' – he'd obviously never heard a Pete Seeger record.

With these accoutrements I would go, sometimes with K, up to this park, where we communed with the solitudes. We started using 'Thoreau' as an incantatory adjective: a certain view of the stream was 'very Thoreau'; the bawling Type A teachers we suffered were certainly not very Thoreau, with the exception of one remarkable guy who took it upon himself to teach the course on literature and ecology – I wonder for how many years *that* has been missing from the curriculum.

The very building of my school in which we were taught Thoreau was demolished several years ago because *more room was needed for the students' cars.*

K and I rode around on our bicycles feeling ecological. Of course we couldn't drive cars yet, so our pretence of making an environmental point was premature. Ecological messages were everywhere at that time (where are they now?). Our thinking hadn't developed far enough to see the absurdity of Californian, *Sand People environmentalism*: slapping a bumper sticker on your CAR that says you love the ecosystem, that you're a member of the Sierra Club. Drop dead!

K was a real mechanic, a woodworker – Thoreau would have liked him. One day we were riding our bikes through huge piles of LEAVES. (In our town the leaves have never had anywhere to go. Japanese gardening helots blow them from one property to another with *gasoline-powered machines*.) But this was a very Thoreau day. Along in a modest VW hatchback came this girl, JODI MENDELSON – whom we both admired – she had been looking possibly quite Thoreau at school today, in a velour jacket of autumn LEAF colours. I coveted JODI and associated her with LEAVES, certainly from this moment; K and I had never discussed girls and if they could be Thoreau or not. (Thoreau had his own problems with girls, I gathered, and I had no wish to emulate him on that score.) But I thought JODI might be the kind of girl to appreciate my Thoreau-like 'fine renouncements'. JODI honked at us, smiled and waved from her car. There, I said, look, JODI – ! Waving! Smiling! K shifted gears as we ploughed into another huge pile of leaves. I think, he said, somewhat subdued, she was smiling at *you*.

Normally (!) I only purchase socks in the autumn, and only in what are usually described as 'autumn colours'. And while I do this I am thinking of that pile of leaves, and JODI. And, of course, Thoreau.

K and I were excited about our Thoreau reading, or half-reading half-extrapolating. To become more environmental, and manlier, we decided to spend a week in the hills and cycle down to school every day. There was a youth hostel at a ranch about twelve miles away. We thought it would be *very* Thoreau. This place was up one of the steepest roads around. We practically killed ourselves getting there, and then the warden was suspicious – he thought we were running away from home. It was very annoying to have to bring up Thoreau and John Muir at the end of a really painful bike ride, when our balls were numb . . . I thought this was the kind of annoyance Thoreau often displayed in his work – flashes of temper – and in person too, I imagined.

To eat we brought cereal with us – 'GRANOLA' – another eco-con job. 'Granola' is a kind of bircher-muesli with added sugar and fruit, and, to judge from the nutritional data, tiny cheeseburgers. It would have been healthier to eat Black Forest cake for breakfast. We had also splurged on a supply of a disgusting dried whole milk – some convenience! – which could only be made up into an assortment of white lumps. Before we fell asleep we talked about JODI, and ANN BEWICK, a girl who kept following K around. In the morning we took our lumps and our cereal, and so down through the hills to school.

I was even sleepier in class than usual, and my legs started to seize up, and tremble, alternately. I realised I couldn't pedal up the hill again, certainly not for a repast of *granola*. K was disappointed, but thought he'd go up there again. We wondered where this was leading. Why had we decided to do this? Me and my *green book*. But I realised I had become frightened that my green book, my boots, chestnut and *Osmiroid* might get dirty, or *rained on*. (Americans have an aversion to rain that is very hard to understand, given the whole history of people getting wet – why should *they* be excused?) ANN came up and started talking to K. She seemed mighty impressed that he was going to ride his 10 SPEED BIKE up and down the hills every day. For how long? 'Ohh – I don't know – ' I think he stuck it that night, and maybe another. Did we try to convince ANN to come with us? And JODI? I went home to hot water and a cooked dinner; I'm not afraid of coming out of this looking like a wimp. K knew how to *use tools*; at that time my Thoreau was all in my head.

What was my little Thoreau ethic for? What was it going to do for ZITS? It was an assemblage of comforting/excoriating ideas, a kind of art I was making. Jung says all art is a search for the father, and my father had grown up in the woods, *real* woods.

Several years later, I was living in the East, experiencing richer autumns. For some reason I was trying to keep very Thoreau in the middle of New York. Sexual inexperience? On a Saturday I would put on my boots and go downtown to a very Thoreau record shop and add to my collection of 'Folkways' LPs. I wandered in Central Park and breathed in the smoke from the gardeners' fires. I rode my bike to the Lower East Side one day in October and brought an enormous PUMPKIN uptown. On my handlebars. Wearing my boots. I cut the pumpkin up into a jack-o'-lantern, put a candle inside, and wrote a poem about it. With my italic pen. But at the same time, this same year, I was poised to discover some civilised (I don't say artificial) essences which Thoreau hated – he'd probably never even heard of some of them: as well as the gardeners' smoke there were the smokes your parents warn you about, the smoke of whiskey and jazz, the smoky skies in the Utrillos in the Modern. The city won, but I always keep him with me. Though *he'd* still prefer to converse with K, I am sure.

A few years later I visited the Thoreau Lyceum, an odd, dear little institution at that time, dedicated to Thoreau's memory in a decided byway of Concord – the town he had so many disagreements with hadn't exactly put him on a pedestal! By the front door was an amusing collection of junk mail addressed to 'Mr Lyceum Thoreau', the result of the place's listing in the telephone book. But in a way, that *was* his name. Didactic? Sure – he had something to say. He stood up and yelled, 'Look out!'

Ansel Adams

The photographer Ansel Adams, who lived all his life in California, brought out many qualities of that state's landscape you might not now associate with it: fog, snow, deserted beaches, clear water. He gave old fences and disused barns a cherishable elegance – fences that weather so artistically, they call attention to themselves, in a way that's become fetishistic. Adams himself has become fetishised. He is become a brand, like everything else, and so has his peculiar vision of California; I'm probably infringing some bloody copyright just by talking about bold clouds, both black and white. Nevertheless there is in his pictures of California the wonderful smell of fog, soil, sage; the chill of wandering into a forest of Coast Redwoods on a warm day.

There is one photograph of his, *Orchard, Santa Clara (the Valley of Heart's Delight!)* taken in the mid-1950s, which propels me back to my childhood; how the world looked from the car. A day in the Californian spring. (It used to rain then.) He had a way of rendering an electric-blue sky in an unmistakable, vibrant grey. The brightness of the tree trunks, the flowers, the fresh rich earth, all spell a certain kind of day in California that has all but disappeared – or perhaps it's the sort of day to which you are only sensitive when young. Adults all stop caring about spring, unless they're Cavalier poets.

Several years ago I was sharing a house in Pacific Grove, the poor man's Carmel, no, the *canny* man's Carmel, with friends from Scotland. Aside from being nonplussed about the town being essentially dry, for outmoded religious reasons, we enjoyed lots of, well, Ansel Adams weather: bright days, foggy evenings, wood fires, walks on the beach, wine . . . (This sounds like a personal ad.) My friend F, a longtime admirer of Adams, and a photographer, was delighted to hear there was an *authorised Ansel Adams gallery* nearby. We cycled there through part of the elegant Del Monte forest on a forenoon straight out of an Adams: bright sun interleaved with the lingering sea fog of the morning. The trees seemed to go on forever in an infinite selection of grey backdrops, yet we could hear the ocean and feel blue heat nearby . . .

While we had expected the *authorised Ansel Adams gallery* to be in some iconoclastic architectural *statement*, or an idiosyncratic, old, holier-than-thou wooden house, it turned out to be one unit in a sort of up-market strip mall. Up-market in that it all appeared to be built of fetishistically weathered birch, and there was no place to park your bike, that is for sure. This *urstripmall* had no video shop or nail salon, but it did boast a shop selling ominously pricey-looking *resort wear*. Resort wear is hard to describe, but let's say it's what Ansel Adams did *not* wear . . .

can you see him climbing on top of his station wagon in a navy blue double-breasted blazer, and a captain's hat with anchors? His pretty assistant in a white over-the-knee pleated skirt piped with gold, and spectator pumps? Yet his photographs had played a role in turning the very place where we were lugubriously standing into a resort, where people now felt they had to buy and wear this weird kind of clothing.

The *authorised gallery* was the sort of place that makes you immediately sweat, every surface designed to gather *your* breath, show *your* fingerprints. The lighting scientifically illustrates *your* failures in shaving and exfoliation. The staff seem like perfect holograms . . . of the SAND PEOPLE. Our sand hologrammatic lassie, in one of those black dresses that does perfect double duty in a gallery and at a cocktail party, welcomed us friendly at first – obviously we were a couple of eccentric millionaires who were spending the morning out of their resort wear. Half the gallery was filled with large map cabinets, in which the authorised Adams pictures reposed, a sleeping army of aesthetic treasure . . . F had a ready answer when asked if he wanted to 'see something' – of course, the *Moonrise over Alamogordo*. Like a nurse, the sand girl put on a pair of muslin gloves which looked like the ones I'd seen among Tutankhamun's effects, only cleaner of course – horrid and surgical while looking soft at the same time. She opened Drawer No. 31-F with the respectful grace of a casket salesman, and disrobed a brilliant silver-gelatin print of that famous image. F gazed down at it, suddenly, with a distinctly *foreign* look, also a slight suggestion that he might drool. As Sand Girl studied us, under the clinical lamps, mixed with 'real' sunshine from outside, if the Monterey Peninsula can any longer be said to have any natural qualities, it occurred to her that she was dealing with a couple of *interlopers*, that there wasn't anything casual about our casualness. What if *Ansel* had wandered in, his beard full of bees and spiders? Her eyes narrowed and the muslin fingers hovered around the turned-back edges of the picture's acid-free negligee.

FS finally managed a polite question – he is nothing if not polite, he's from Edinburgh – his mother would have taught him it is polite to ask the price. 'These prints are fifteen thousand dollars,' she said, or something like that – even I, who'd been struggling to live with Californian excess for some years, was taken aback, suddenly much more interested in my bike and what was going on in the parking lot. 'Is this a real possibility for you?' she said – one of the most frightening, and rude, questions I've ever heard. 'Absolutely not,' came FS's gasping answer. It sounded like she'd stood on his chest.

Back through the pines; couple beers; the landscape *different* – the *richesse* of Ansel's disappearing, unbeknownst to him of course.

Cucamonga

The war was over and the city was bright. It was angular, shed of its Buicky big band bulges, yet it was colourful, appealing, energetic. New, stylised trees were suggested with penwork, freely splashed with greens. Trolley cars streamed past the stout red hydrants, in front of clean shops, under gay banners hoisted across the boulevard: WELCOME CONVENTIONEERS. WELCOME, WELCOME. Traffic was heavy, to judge by the violins. Look at it from my point of view. I was a pig. I stuttered.

I took my bag and walked around, the pavement hard under my hooves. The hotels were all full. On Third Street even a banner taped inside the flyblown window of Fred's Flophouse: *G'WAN – BEAT IT!* On Wilshire an entire block had been levelled and signs announced 1,000 ROOM HOTEL TO BE ERECTED ON THIS SITE. And there, standing in line, were a thousand faceless numbskulls, their hats, their briefcases. Things were tough. I peeked into the cool garden of a house. There was a perfect dog house, *the classic* dog house, FIDO painted over the arched door. This canine saw me and hung out a NO VACANCY sign. Disgusted, I went back downtown.

I was walking past the Biltmore, where I'd already tried, n-natch, when suddenly this Franklin Pangborn type rushes out on to the sidewalk, from nowhere whips out a ROOM FOR RENT sign and tears back inside. In less than a second they were upon him. Hundreds of arms and legs, briefcases and hats were trying to get in. He was pushing the door against us as hard as he could. I was the one that made it. He told me the room was on the thirtieth floor and I'd have to share. He mopped his brows, which imitated his moustache in worry, with a huge handkerchief he pulled from his hotel manager's tail-coat. I wasn't about to complain.

I walked across the lobby, a huge perfectly mauve pool of carpeting, past an improbable number of repeating potted palms. It was the giant, everywhere-lobby. The elevator boy was that long-armed drooping fellow from all the hotels I ever stayed in. The door closed and we shot up thirty storeys in one second. Darkness, my hat on my hooves.

It was the standard, everywhere-hotel room, with everywhere-hotel furniture that would repeat, in a chase. But this was no time to be thinking about that. On the bureau was a large photograph in an easel frame. I picked it up. It was of a queer, assertive-looking duck with big, come-on eyes and a slightly spiky haircut. Must be my roommate. I told myself he looked OK. Always hoping for the best. I was beat. I went into the closet and came out immediately in my nightshirt. I hope he will come in quietly, I said to myself as I put out the light.

I still don't know what the hour was when the door crashed

open like gunfire and an insane, inebriated voice was singing the kind of song you sing when you're drunk in a hotel. He turned on the light and marched through the room. This was the guy in the picture! He jumped up on the bed. I tried to hide behind the sheets but he snatched them away. He sang, loudly and directly, into my face. He jumped madly about the bed, then leapt on to the metal rail at the foot. He said he was glad to meet me. He then began to chant, spelling out some guy's name, the chant becoming so fast it sounded like a train and the next thing he was chugging rapidly back and forth on the foot of the bed, using his arms like the drive rods of a locomotive, smoke belching from a cigar that appeared from nowhere in his bill, all this culminating in the wild ultimation of his scream. I shouted back, no longer afraid of this lunatic but determined to get to the bottom of the situation, so as to get to sleep. I asked him what the hell he was talking about. He dropped his cigar, flustered, WC Fields-like. I asked him again, calmly, who this character was. He said he was a kangaroo, a six-foot invisible kangaroo. So that was it. Delirium tremens. The thought of having to deal with this all night made me angry. Suddenly he appeared to unzip something in thin air and to my amazement he climbed in and disappeared. Only his mad head was visible and it proceeded to bounce around the room. He asked me indignantly how I thought he was accomplishing this, if there were no invisible kangaroo. Then he jumped out of whatever it was and confronted me. He said I'd hurt his friend's feelings.

I was determined to get some sleep that night. Told him I still didn't believe him. He walked towards the door, making comradely gestures in thin air, saying he'd see the guy tomorrow. He shut the door and came towards the bed. I pretended to have settled already. He grumbled about my manners. He got into bed, remarking on my embonpoint. Not wishing to start anything fresh, I ignored this and merely murmured *Buenos noches* in Spanish as I regularly jocularly do. And put out the light. I remember there was moonlight on the bedframe.

The light came on. He asked me what I'd meant. I said, Spanish for *bon soir*. He was satisfied and put off the light. He put on the light. Rapped on my skull for entry. What did *that* mean? Now confused and further hurt I told him it was French in place of the Spanish. He gave me a vague look and put out the light. Instantly though he put it on again, took a brass alarm clock from under his pillow, hammered me on the head with it, then tossed it aside as I fought and spluttered awake. Then he told me to forget it. And put out the light. He rose immediately and walked to the front of the bed where there was a crank, which I had assumed was for raising and lowering the head, if you wanted to read. He turned it rapidly, and as I fully came to, the bed coughed, choked, and started up like a car, vibrating horribly. He climbed in beside me as we rattled up and down, a terrific grin on his face. The bed bucked, leapt about and backfired, then wheezed to a stop. He shrugged at me and looked around wildly. He said he thought we were out of gas. I turned away, annoyed. He put out the light.

Incredible hiccuping began instantaneously. Again he put the goddamn light on; he reached across me for my glass of water and drank *gep gep gep* and was then asleep. He had however dumped the rest of the water on me – which at first I took with loathing to be enuresis. I clamped the empty tumbler over his snoring bill. I put out the light. No sooner had I done so than all the bedclothes were ripped away from my body. I turned on the light. He was wrapped snugly. I whipped back my share and turned off the light. But again the blankets were immediately snatched from me. I put on the light. He had all the covers. I took back what was rightfully mine and turned off the light. Yet AGAIN were they yanked away, though this time I held on to one blanket with my teeth. But when I turned on the light I found to my fury that I was biting only a little scrap of it. He had the rest. This time I took them all, and turned off the light.

Instantly came the human castanet sound of chattering teeth. He put on the light, staring in horror at his feet, which were immobilised in huge *blocks of ice*. But before I could derive any satisfaction from his discomfort he lifted the bedclothes and jammed his feet against my naked flesh. I shrieked and flew upwards, bringing him with me, as was our wont. We landed by the window. I seized him and began to stuff him into a pillowcase, telling him exactly what I thought of him. He held his head in dismay at my righteous litany, objecting only to one particularly insulting term. In answer I took the pillowcase containing him to the open window and let it fall to the street. There was that quick jet plane sound of rapid descent and then the crash. The one with leather sofa cushions, bass drum, cymbals, symphonic gong, and the glass crashbox. I walked back to bed. I regretted this of course – he was a perfect stranger to me. But I needed sleep. I got in bed and began snoring theatrically. Fifteen years earlier they would have put up one of the sawing logs.

He was observing me coolly from the window sill, covered in professional bandages and on crutches, looking resigned. In a convulsion he shook off these appliances and pulled down the window shade, decorated with a naïve scene, the sun rising across a farmyard. It was getting light. He crowed, like a rooster, then rushed over and stood stiffly next to my head. He loudly imitated a large alarm clock ticking and then ringing. I woke. He hideously extended his bill, trumpety, and began blaring out *Reveille*. I got out of bed . . .

I was stunned, half asleep. He led me in calisthenics and I groggily obeyed. After only three or four squat thrusts he propelled me towards the closet, saying I would be late for my train. Somehow this made sense. I quickly folded all my clothes into one suitcase. I took it and made towards him, as he was now wearing a conductor's cap, standing stiffly at the window. Under the sill he had placed a Pullman step. I walked up the step and disappeared out the window.

But I made the train. The train leaving from outside our room on the thirtieth floor. The whistle blew and we began to pull out and I saw him raise the shade in astonishment. I waved to him from inside my unmistakably *turista* Hawaiian shirt. Did I hear him murmur this was silly?

Babbitt

To the American public irony has become unintelligible.
EDITH WHARTON, after the publication of *Babbitt*

You can't read *Babbitt* without feeling uneasy, and sad, without slapping yourself in the forehead – without wishing that things could be much, much better, wishing away our 'leaders' and their errant Babbittry. The critic Filson Young wrote, 'a world inhabited by Sinclair Lewis's characters would be a nightmare'. Lewis suggested that nightmare in 1922, and now we're living it. After George Santayana read *Babbitt* he asked, 'is America really so helpless and distracted?' Yup. Or as George Follansbee Babbitt himself would say, 'Yump.'

Babbitt, like *Walden*, is a vital American book you don't see around the classroom much any more. Yet for years I have thought that you need read only *Babbitt* if you would understand the United States, that is the United States that began to decline so quickly after its inception. Everything Sinclair Lewis predicted for my country, in the nicest possible way, finally and perhaps unchangeably has come true. With the slack apathy sprayed over us like insect repellent by Reagan and Bush, the pounding, unnatural, unilateral, dull voice of business triumphed. Is no one ever going to get up from his sofa and television again?

After Reagan was elected I read *Babbitt* with new eyes; I staggered around wondering how something so *clairvoyant* could have fallen from consciousness – hadn't everyone read *Babbitt* in high school English class? And if so, how could they have elected, how can they keep on electing, keep on *becoming* these guys?

The businessmen who drive Zenith, the Midwestern city of 300,000 where *Babbitt* takes place, constantly pester each other with the question, 'Don't you think it's time we had a *real business administration?*', the nauseated italics mine. (It means they want a laissez-faire Republican executive and Congress in Washington.) Reagan used to go on and *on* about 'unchaining the private sector', which we used to laugh at, at the time, since the private sector seemed to be doing quite enough damage. But my hat's off to him – guess they *were* sorta over-regulated – 'cause look what we've got *now*. Republicans won't ever listen to any regulatory talk, because we live in an overpopulated, polluted, corrupt, dirty, debased, dangerous society – and that's the way they like it. They make money out of it being that way. Aww: anyway, 'these reform cranks always exaggerate,' as Babbitt grouses.

Babbitt gives a speech to the Zenith real-estate board: 'Some time I hope folks will stop giving credit to a lot of moth-eaten, mildewed, out-of-date, old, European dumps . . . believe me, the world has fallen too long for these worn-out countries that aren't producing anything but bootblacks and scenery and booze, that haven't got one bathroom per hundred people . . .' How is it *possible* that Sinclair Lewis was a speech writer for Donald Rumsfeld?

Lewis's accuracy, sympathy and irony of observation, his humour and poetry in language dangles the United States before you like one of the odd signposts you encounter on the outskirts of American towns of a certain size and outlook, a display of medallions and shields, awards on the chest of the town. These plywood and sheet-metal honours tell you which churches, business groups, and even secret societies (guardedly) *Welcome You To . . .*

. . . *ZENITH?* Lewis was already appalled at the rapidly growing *sameness* of so many places in America. Later in life he claimed Thoreau as a hero of his. He actually wasn't sounding tip-top when he made this claim, but there are similarities between the two, in their angry wistfulness about what might have been, if their countrymen would only take advantage of freedom, instead of driving forward an insane, fearful mania to insulate and conform. What is amusing is that shortly after the publication of *Babbitt* a number of cities including Cincinnati, Duluth, Kansas City, Milwaukee and Minneapolis all rushed forward with claims *to be Zenith*. If they'd thought about it a little more they might not have immediately demanded this distinction. It's a city with no real future except that of commerce; you get the feeling that one of these years it could turn into the mercenary 'Pottersville', the fantastical fate of Bedford Falls in Frank Capra's *It's a Wonderful Life* when the evil banker manages to oust the Baileys from their (commie!) Building and Loan.

The intellectual integrity, if not the moral, of Babbitt and his conscience is confronted by a series of strikes and union marches. He's been fooling around with some low arty types in a vain attempt to 'see life' lately: 'Don't you love to sit on the floor? It's so Bohemian!' a culture-vulture brays at him at a party. For a while, he can see nothing more enchanting. Babbitt doesn't immediately express the contempt for these labourite activities expected of him by his business club cronies (the 'Boosters'). He's bullied by his own sullied confusion into attending church:

> . . . the Chatham Road Presbyterian Church announced a sermon by Dr John Jennison Drew on "How the Savior Would End Strikes." Babbitt had been negligent about church-going lately, but went to the service, hopeful that Dr Drew really did have the information as to what the divine powers thought about strikes.

This religious worthy, really only a businessman in disguise, tells his flock:

> I certainly am criticizing the systems in which the free and fluid motivation of independent labor is to be replaced with cooked-up wage scales and minimum salaries and government commissions and labor federations and all that poppycock. What is not generally understood is that

this whole industrial matter isn't a question of economics. It's essentially and only a matter of Love, and of the practical application of the Christian religion!

What could bode any worse, or more accurately, for all those not 'privileged' to be in the Zenith Athletic Club, to be Boosters? And could anything ring the big Bush bell of doom more ponderously? To his credit Babbitt refuses to believe this stuff, for the moment. But his liberalism is short-lived. His most lucrative real-estate deals, often made with insider information, are *sub-rosa*, not to say downright illegal. Eventually he's pressed back into the flock of corrupt, small-town networkers by the very real fear that they can ruin his business, not taking his advertising and steering customers to other brokers.

The publication of *Babbitt* has been credited with the rapid growth of the neologism 'realtor', which Babbitt's enthusiasm for is roundly mocked by Lewis. (HL Mencken quoted a joke about two new pretentious words making the rounds: 'What is a *mortician*? A *mortician* is a man that buries a *realtor*.')

The Midwest back-slapping, bridge-party racism is here. Babbitt and his pals worry constantly about the black man becoming 'uppity', and Lewis, always alive to bigotry, even shows how the desperate economic need to 'fit in' has a Booster with a Jewish surname using anti-Semitic expressions, and a Jewish comedian who makes 'vicious fun of Jews'. In a smoky, late-night bull session on a train, one of Lewis's endless travelling loudmouths proclaims, 'These Dagoes and Hunkies have got to learn that this is a white man's country, and they ain't wanted here. When we've assimilated the foreigners we got here now and learned 'em the principles of Americanism and turned 'em into regular folks, why then maybe we'll let in a few more.' What the word *folks* has become today, especially in Republican Washington! Mark the chillingly cute name for the agency of assimilation in Philip Roth's *The Plot Against America:* 'Just Folks'.

The American Protestant's religious muddle is amusingly sketched, the competition between the denominations shown to be nothing more than corporations rivalling each other for custom. Evangelists take their lumps, though smaller lumps than they got in Lewis's *Elmer Gantry*. And there are marvellous precursors of such modern wackinesses for the swanky gullible as Scientology. Myra Babbitt, both in an attempt to get her husband back on some kind of moral foothold and to stake some little rebellion against the straitened society the women of Zenith particularly feel, takes him to hear the Dickensian-named Mrs Opal Emerson Mudge, the promulgator of 'the New Thought', and the editor of *Pearls of Healing* magazine:

Most of the men slouched in their chairs and wriggled, while their wives sat rigidly at attention, but two of them – red-necked, meaty men – were as respectably devout as their wives. They were newly rich contractors who, having bought houses, motors, hand-painted pictures, and gentlemanliness, were now buying a refined ready-made philosophy. It had been a toss-up with them whether to

buy New Thought, Christian Science, or a good standard
high-church model of Episcopalianism.

Babbitt rebels later on the way home, Myra having reproached
him by saying she thinks taking a stab at metaphysics is better
than people 'going to roadhouses and smoking and drinking'.
Babbitt: 'I don't know whether it is or not! Personally I don't see
a whole lot of difference. In both cases they're trying to get away
from themselves – most everybody is, these days, I guess.' Even
then, the pervasive, sometimes hysterical sense that Americans,
American men in particular, were at least subconsciously horrified
at what they were creating and were desperate to escape from it.
Much deeper than the political, *Babbitt* is most essentially about
what an awful thing it is to be a man – how awful that there must
be such creatures at all, let alone that they're in charge – especially
when so baffled in the face of the physical universe they're in
the process of making. Some savvy soul in Cleveland Ohio gave
a talk shortly after the novel was published entitled 'Babbitt:
a Challenge to Men', and it certainly is, though most teachers
don't put it that way. For a goodly period after it appeared it was
treated with contempt in civic forums and, of course, at pulpits,
even like something seditious. Does that not mark it as a work of
art worthy of our respect?

When we first meet Babbitt he is grumpily being awakened
from erotic dreams, with a hangover: 'It was the best of nationally
advertised and quantitatively produced alarm-clocks, with all
modern attachments, including cathedral chime, intermittent

alarm and a phosphorescent dial. Babbitt was proud of being awakened by such a rich device. Socially it was almost as credible as buying expensive cord tires.' We follow him into the bath, his frustrated and immediate male morning rage giving the opportunity for one of the great slapstick scenes in modern fiction – despite the luxurious appointments of his nearly-new bathroom, his razor blade is dull, he gets soap in his eyes, he grabs at towel after towel (they're all wet, having already been used by the family), finally taking the unbelievable step of using THE GUEST TOWEL, something never, ever done in American homes.

For some time Babbitt has been eyeing up a cigar-lighter to install on the dashboard of his car. (There's a funny *Confessions of Zeno*-style battle with himself about smoking through the story.) He's ashamed of the expense, but takes the opportunity to stage a perfect little act of male hostility and self-justification. Driving to work he calculates his income, expenses and worth, working himself into a fit, even though he's doing rather well:

'Right up at the top of the heap! But – Way expenses are – Family wasting petrol, and always dressed like millionaires, and sending that eighty a month to Mother – And all these stenographers and salesmen gouging me for every cent they can get – ' The effect of his scientific budget-planning was that he felt at once triumphantly wealthy and perilously poor, and in the midst of these dissertations he stopped his car, rushed into a small news-and-miscellany shop, and bought the electric cigar-lighter which he had coveted for a week. He dodged his conscience by being jerky and noisy, and by shouting at the clerk, 'Guess this will prett' near pay for itself in matches, eh?'

Preparing for a trip to Maine with his oldest friend, a man who doesn't participate in the bouncy mercantile emptiness of Zenith, Babbitt goes nuts in the camping-equipment store, partly because he's looking forward to getting away from his family, partly because he's a red-blooded American male who just *loves stuff*:

> He trumpeted and danced . . . he gloated on fly-rods and gorgeous rubber hip-boots, on tents with celluloid windows and folding chairs and ice-boxes. He simple-heartedly wanted to buy all of them . . . 'Oh I guess old Mr Trout won't come a hustling when I drop one of those red ants on the water!' asserted Babbitt, and his thick wrists made a rapturous motion of casting.

Clock, up-to date shaving-mirror, car, cigar-lighter, fishing-rod, his luxurious neckties – all these things drive him crazy. They are ungraspable symbols *of something*. Babbitt will never be sure what – manliness? Power? They will never reveal their true nature to him because, as one astute critic of *Babbitt* wrote, in America 'there is no civilisation for the equipment'. The (often painfully funny) frustration Babbitt experiences at the hands of this equipment anticipates the deliberately thing-shunning men in the fiction of Beckett. Watt and Murphy have brought men a little way forward. But perhaps only themselves.

Nature itself, the grandiloquent, fulsome American-out-of doors, perhaps already fetishised beyond use in 1922, fails to satisfy him in the end. He's conversing by a beautiful lake with the romantic figure of Joe Paradise, his guide:

> He sat on a stump and felt virile. 'Joe, what would you do if you had a lot of money? Would you stick to guiding, or would you take a claim 'way back in the woods and be independent of people?' For the first time Joe brightened. He chewed his cud a second and bubbled, 'I've often thought of that! If I had the money I'd go down to Tinker's Falls and open a swell shoe store.'

Always at cross-purposes, these men of ours. The natural world is perhaps the most poignant of the many things that slip through Babbitt's chubby fingers.

One of his many erroneous opinions about himself is, of course, that he not only knows how the world works, but that he's a man of the world. His blundering attempts at 'other women' in the story become increasingly frantic and awful. In the spirit of Prohibition, he and his cronies assume that certain mild liberties can be theirs, always of course under the bullshitty moral umbrellas provided by their various professions, lodges, booster groups and so on. This is the wan but insistent patriarchy of the inter-war period. ('Oh, you righteous men! How wicked you are! How rotten wicked!' one woman is driven to say, after her frustrated husband has *shot her*.) A number of wives in the novel are depicted as being slightly unhinged as they have literally nothing to do except make house (though most have a maid, at least) and shop. None of the husbands will allow them even to do any voluntary work of consequence because they're terrified of *creeping socialism*. The double standards used by Babbitt's crowd with regard to Prohibition ring true today with regard to the United States attitude to South America and its virtually *necessary* supply of drugs. While downing dreadful cocktails made sometimes with 'pre-war gin', sometimes with poisonous bathtub hooch, they pontificate more and more loudly about how Prohibition keeps *working men* on the straight and narrow, while they, the sensible, enlightened ones, may of course enjoy a drink – their due *as men*. (When they can't drink, what they really like to do is get together and *swear*.)

Lewis writes of the women of Zenith: 'the strange thing is that the longer one knew the women, the less alike they seemed; while the longer one knew the men, the more alike their bold patterns appeared.' Babbitt's first flirtation is with Louetta Swanson, a pretty neighbour with perhaps the loudest, most boring husband among all these boring men. Drawing her on to the veranda during a party, Babbitt paws her a little. She allows herself to be clumsily embraced, but when he moves to kiss her she utters a chillingly mechanical 'Don't'. His next attempt is on the person of Ida Putiak: 'the girl who especially disturbed him – though he had never spoken to her – was the last girl on the right in the Pompeian Barber Shop . . . she wore thin salmon-colored blouses which exhibited her shoulders and her black-ribboned camisoles.' After flirting with her like any meat-head businessman, and nervously enquiring about other meat-head businessmen who must get 'fresh' all the time, he gets her out to a secluded roadhouse and buys her a gross platter of dinner made the more grotesque by his tongue-tied lovemaking. (He reminds you of the great Ned Beatty in *Nashville* – Beatty was born to play Babbitt. We're over-regulated, that's for sure!) In the taxi on the way back she dodges him expertly for her nineteen years: 'Just sit back, dearie, and see what a swell night it is. If you're a good boy, maybe I'll kiss you when we say nighty-night. Now give me a cigarette.' And Tanis Judique, the sympathetic widow with whom he does eventually conduct an affair when his wife is out of town, is even better defended with her cigarette, managing during their early courtship always to have one lighted when he wishes to take her hand in his.

All these women live in Zenith, the same morally confused American city that he does, but with the difference that they also live in the real world, a jigsaw of misplaced sexuality invented and controlled by realtors, coal dealers, cheap preachers, aristocratic bankers and hollow advertising men. Babbitt longs for the 'not impossible she who would understand him, value him, make him happy.' They're always complaining that they're misunderstood, men, but what in Hell is so hard to understand?

Look: they are what they are. Look at what they made. When a man says no one understands him, he *definitely* means he can't understand himself.

When riled, that is, cornered, whether by wife or mistress, we see in Babbitt that 'as in many men the cringing of a dog, the flinching of a frightened child, rouse not pity but a surprised and jerky cruelty' – Myra has it out with him about Tanis, and Babbitt is on true male form, a misguided missile of white-hot self-aggrandisement:

> With true masculine wiles he not only convinced himself that she had injured him, but, by the loudness of his voice and the brutality of his attack, he convinced her also, and presently he had her apologizing for his having spent the evening with Tanis. He went up to bed well pleased, not only the master but the martyr of the household.

For years Babbitt has dreamt of a 'fairy child' who softly comes to him, comforts and loves him, and to whom he sometimes ascribes the face of whatever woman is occupying his non-thoughts at the moment. He's an emotional ringer for Dr Chumley in *Harvey*. Poor thing. Poor, poor thing. (The Dowds would fit into Zenith quite well. Perhaps they're already there.)

In the end Babbitt collapses back into the absolute worst possible hypocrisies of his existence: 'all of them believed that American Democracy did not imply any equality of wealth, but did demand a wholesome sameness of thought, dress, painting, morals and vocabulary'. Like Winston Smith in *1984*, he loves Big Brother. Or Big Booster.

Much as Arthur Miller's *The Crucible*, *Babbitt* is a scary tale of a plausible oligarchy, something Americans are too happy to be getting on with. It's also a lament for a ubiquitous education which might have set everyone free, this in the nation which gave to the world (and has now severely crippled) the institution of the free public high school. One of *Babbitt*'s suitably alarmed early readers despaired that 'no suggestion of the direction appears in which salvation may come'. What about learning?

Harvey

I've *wrestled with reality for thirty-five years, Doctor, and I'm
happy to state that I finally won out over it.* So, enviably, Elwood
P Dowd, the almost supernaturally incisive eccentric in Mary
Chase's devastating study of American repression and denial.
Ostensibly a dark comedy about a meek bachelor with an invisible
pal (a six-foot rabbit that wears hats and overcoats), *Harvey* is
not about the rabbit at all, despite some goofy theatrical tricks
aimed at convincing the audience that he exists in a pantomime-
ghost way. *Elwood* is the other-worldly spirit of the piece (I'm
speaking of the stage play and the film interchangeably), a subtle,
mischief-making goblin dropped by an angry sky-god straight
down into the middle of the middle class in an overly ordered
middle America.

The dialogue of *Harvey*, the (very) social fabric of the play,
is polite speech itself – the constant, unthinking exchange
of pleasantries in this homogenous group of people *mired in
politeness*. It can seem that *all* the dialogue is *How do you do,
I'm glad to know you, let me give you one of my cards* . . . The
repressed lives in this town of 'the far West' (Mary Chase was

139

from Denver – in the film things look a bit more Midwestern, it could almost be Zenith), the longing for something else, another *kind* of world, seep continuously from the interstices of this talk. *Myrtle Mae Simmons!*, exclaims Elwood's sister Veta at a crucial moment, *You've got a lot to learn – and I hope you never learn it!* It's a little like Swift's brutal *Polite Conversation* of 1738, in which he constructs a damning picture of the non-thought in the best society through little dialogues which, though realistic, are made up only of clichés, proverbs and 'received ideas'.

Elwood Dowd is a *bomb* thrown into this museum, no, *mausoleum* of propriety. Did he awake one morning in early middle age and decide to re-make America, turn society on its head? To base it on love? He is a constant, assiduous leveller. He was *born to blur*, blur the hypocritical distinctions of niceness that America depends on.

So many shrewdly-used psychoanalytic ideas underpin *Harvey* – an important one is the fear of what is INSIDE being brought OUTSIDE, and vice-versa. Elwood constantly invites home to dinner people he meets in bars and runs into on the street, to the consternation of Veta – people who simply don't exist in her conception of the town. Elwood has set himself to do this, and there may be an element of sadism in it. While not overtly sinister about it, Elwood allows himself to enjoy for a moment or two the idea that the shrinks think *Veta* is the maniac. In his personality there is something of the dreamy arsonist, whom you wouldn't be surprised to discover gently beaming down from a hillside on the inferno he's caused below.

Elwood crusades against the over-compartmentalisation of life, which plagues the western world. Why shouldn't you invite people you meet by chance to dinner? What is friendship? How and why does it occur, and what is one really supposed to do with it once it is recognised to exist? In order to get the people in his life to ask themselves these questions, he injects a strange, Zen-like slowness into his encounters with everyone. His deadpan, expectantly probing responses to ordinary usages tossed off by the others have the effect of flustering them even further about his presence. When Veta tells him she'd *like to talk to him*, using the phrase as people do to warn him that she has something important and unpleasant to say (that she wants to commit him to a mental institution), Elwood comes back with *Well, I'd like to talk to you too, Veta – I've got some spare time and you're welcome to all of it*. He's able to counter any *threat* (he's fully aware of the forces gathering against him) with a super-concentrated *parody* of the falsity surrounding him.

Underneath all the politeness, there's the roller coaster of eros, and Elwood has appointed himself to remind everyone of this wherever possible. When anyone asks him what they can do for him, his response is always *What did you have in mind?* Elwood has an erotic life, or at least a life of erotic longing. He assiduously flirts with the nurses in the sanatorium, with the wife of the chief psychiatrist Dr Chumley, takes an interest in women sitting across the bar and also enjoys playing cupid, between doctor and nurse and between his niece Myrtle Mae and Marvin, the bruiser of an orderly who's always yanking him offstage. He is more than interested in the idea that Dr Chumley has 'affairs', even though the word was used only in the business sense. Although at first it hardly seems so, Elwood usually interjects a tiny, hazy spiciness into any conversation. Veta has tried to commit him to the asylum, but has been locked up herself because she has described too vividly the trials of living with Elwood and the rabbit (it doesn't help that she is wearing one of the daftest hats you have ever seen). The *ingénu* shrink Dr Sanderson tries to apologise to Elwood for having wrongfully detained him, saying he and the young nurse Kelly have *made a mistake out here this afternoon*. Elwood insists on misinterpreting this as an admission of hanky-panky and milks it for everything it's worth in a perverse, Freudian burlesque (there is an earthy element of *ba-dum-bump!* in the play as well as its polished satire). Sanderson tells him that the fault was all his and Elwood replies *Your attitude may be old-fashioned, Doctor, but I like it.* There's next a socko joke when Sanderson says *Now if I had seen your sister first, that would have been an entirely different matter.*

With his intense, weird friendliness, Elwood attempts to drag the young doctor and nurse from their milieu into his – 'downtown' (a chilling word in America), to Charlie's Place: *And the four of us will spend a very pleasant evening together.* The fourth being, of course, Harvey, who is not so much a drunk's hallucination or imaginary companion as he is the earthly name for the emotional life that's missing around here. But being a brilliantly conceived 'object', Harvey stands for one thing and then another, depending on how firmly one believes in him. (The action of the play is the progress of each character more or less tacitly acknowledging Harvey's existence; in the end even Dr Chumley is charmed by him.) Hence the perfect description of him as a pooka, a mischievous Celtic spirit – though this definition applies just as aptly to Elwood.

The town Elwood and Veta live in is a wonderful construction of Chase's – with just a few hints you understand the interconnectedness, the *lack of air* against which Elwood has quietly but firmly set his existence. It's a world which was also deftly rendered by Helen Hokinson, one of the great cartoonists of the *New Yorker* magazine. The afternoon tea party scene in *Harvey*, especially in the filmed version, complete with fur stole-wearing pianiste and frighteningly jiggly-bosomed amateur soprano ('*Hop hop hop hop hippity hop, o'er the golden sea . . .*') is a Hokinson drawing come to life. It's said repeatedly that Elwood 'could have made something of himself'; Veta exasperatedly tells him at one point that he *could be sitting on the Western Slope Water Board* if only he'd go over and ask them. Dr Chumley exists on the same social level as Judge Gaffney, Veta's longtime admirer and protector. The spread of *names* says much about the place: the old-established feel of Dowd, Simmons, Gaffney; the underlings Kelly, Lofgren, Meigles and Schimmelpletzer; Veta's matronly friends Mrs Halsey, Mrs Tewkesbury, Ethel Chauvenet. Elwood spends his afternoons downtown in Charlie's Place, Blondie's Chicken Inn, Eddie's . . . (Sanderson asks Veta if Elwood drinks 'to excess' and she replies *Well, don't you call it excess when a man never lets a day go by without stepping into one of those cheap taverns, sitting around with riffraff and people you've never heard of?*) The names in *Harvey* are redolent of the middle Western hierarchies, of *Babbitt*.

It's almost impossible to conceive of how *Harvey* might have come into existence without the talents of Josephine Hull, who created the role of Veta on Broadway and carried her into the film, frantically hitching up her girdle all the way. She begins the scenario in a state of high anxiety and manages to crank it up scene by scene until she becomes totally hysterical, expressing fear for everything in the world and then some; finally she cracks completely and attempts to rescue Elwood from the jaws of psychiatry, where she firmly believed he belonged (before she herself was stripped naked and dunked in a hydrotherapy tub by the indefatigable, acerbic Marvin). There are deft mirrorings throughout the play, levelling devices worthy of Elwood himself: he suggests kindly that Veta should sign the papers for her own commitment – *Veta always does all the signing in our family* – and so stands the process on its head. *She* later wistfully longs for his protection upon escaping the asylum (*Wait till Elwood hears what they did to me, he won't stand for it!*) at the same time that she's trying to get him thrown in permanently. At the end of her tether, Veta begs to be allowed to go upstairs to her own bed where she can *LET GO!*

To his obvious delight, Elwood finally does succeed in turning absolutely everything upside down. In the role of analyst he listens to the recumbent Dr Chumley's fantasies (these involve

a 'quiet woman', beer, and two weeks at a motel in Akron, Ohio
– she's to stroke his hand and say *Poor thing, poor, poor thing*).
This little soliloquy gives full expression to everything Elwood
wants dragged out into the open. The question Elwood P Dowd
poses to everyone, to *America*, is: what life will you lead? The
AFFECTIVE life, or that of DUTY? The town has got away
in the past with characterising him as a crackpot, that is to say,
an amiable, 'functional alcoholic'. The American abjuration of
drinking, of bars, is the protestant attitude towards the inner life.
American bars (most of which never had windows – what was
'inside' should stay 'inside') stand for what is illicit in America:
the emotions. They are the shady headquarters for all those who
would listen to the tom-toms of the id. And for that they have
always been shamed. In American thought you only drink if you
have some kind of BIG PROBLEM. *Nobody ever brings anything
small into a bar*, says Elwood. But Charlie's Place, in the film
of *Harvey*, is also the only place where you see people enjoying
themselves. In all the smoke there is much more air than at Veta's
tea party or the sanatorium.

*Doctor, when I was a little boy, my mother used to say to me,
'Elwood' – she always called me 'Elwood' – 'as you go through
life you must be either "oh, so smart," or "oh, so pleasant."' For
years – I was smart. I recommend pleasant. You may quote me.*
Harvey is a surprising mid-twentieth-century *plea* for weirdness,
individuality, for *kindness*, a vote for a necessary biodiversity of
personalities, a society of emotional richness that might have
succeeded that of the unsatisfactory, self-satisfied striving and

self-strangulation that always defined life in America. If people won't read Freud they could at least read *Harvey*, a perfectly poised piece of American ambiguity. You leave it feeling like one of those tippy rocks in the desert – as if you might balance on a needlepoint for hundreds of years to come.

Cary Grant's Suit

*N*orth by Northwest isn't about what happens to Cary Grant, it's about what happens to his *suit*. The suit has the adventures, a gorgeous New York suit threading its way through America. The title sequence in which the stark lines of a Madison Avenue office building are 'woven' together could be the construction of Cary in his suit right there – he gets knitted into his suit, into his job, before our very eyes. Indeed some of the popular 'suitings' of that time, 'windowpane' or 'glen plaid', perfectly complemented office buildings. Cary's suit reflects New York, identifies him as a thrusting exec, but also arms him, protects him, what else is a suit for? *Reflects and Protects* . . . a slogan Roger Thornhill himself might have come up with.

But, as Thoreau wrote, 'a man who has at length found something to do will not need to get a new suit to do it in'. Cary may cut quite a figure, but as a person he is meaningless, so far. We find him in the suit, but certainly he has not found himself, or 'what to do'.

The recent idiom of calling a guy a 'suit' if you don't like him, consider him a flunky or a waste of space, applies to Cary at the beginning of the film: this *suit* comes barrelling out of the elevator, yammering business trivialities a mile a minute, almost with the energy of the entire building. The suit moves with its secretary into the hot evening sun where we can get a good look at it: it's a real beaut, a perfectly-tailored, gracefully-falling lightweight dusty blue – it might be a gown, you know. It's fun to think of it as 'dusty' blue because of what befalls it later. It's by far the best suit in the movie, in the *movies*, perhaps the whole world. The villains, James Mason and Martin Landau, wear suits of funereal, sinister (though sleek and pricey) black, while their greasy henchmen run around in off-the-peg browny crap. 'The Professor', head of Intelligence, bumbles about in pipe-smoked tweed and a revolting shirt of old-mannie *blue*.

In 1959 we were a white shirt and black suit nation: the 'revolution' if you want to dignify it that way, was ten years off. There's a nice photograph of Ernest Lehman, who wrote this picture, sitting in Hitchcock's office, a typically late-1950s black and white office, natty in a white shirt and narrow black tie. Some could make this look good but if you were *forced* to dress this way, say if you worked for IBM, it contributed only to the general gloominess of the age. Sometimes you can find yourself wondering if life itself was conducted in colour then – even the 'summer of love' was largely photographed in black and white. Don't let anyone kid you: the sixties were dreary.

Outside on Madison there, the white shirts blind you, but not a none of them is quite so white as Cary's. (Even as someone with experience in theatrical make-up, I have no idea how they kept it off these white, white collars. It drives me nuts.) Non-streaky Cary's daring and dashing in the most amazing suit in New York. His silk tie is exactly one shade darker than the suit, his socks exactly one shade lighter. In the cab he tells his secretary to remind him to 'think thin', which allows us to regard his suit, how it lies on his physique.

A friend of mine in politics said to me once, 'I love wearing suits. They're like pyjamas. You can go around all day doing business in your pyjamas.' It has to be said that his suits were pretty nice, particularly so for *Boston*; whether he meant that he did his business half-asleep only his constituents could say.

The suit, Cary inside it, strides with confidence into the Plaza Hotel. Nothing bad happens to it until one of the greasy henchmen grasps Cary by the shoulder. *We're already in love with this suit* and it feels like a real violation. They bundle him into a cab and shoot out to Long Island, not much manhandling yet. In fact Martin Landau is impressed: 'He's a well-tailored one, isn't he?' *He* loves the suit. But next Cary tries to escape, there's a real struggle, they force all that bourbon down his throat . . . (He later thinks they'll find liquor stains on the sofa, but if there was that much violence why aren't there any on the suit?) Cut to Cary being stuffed into the Mercedes-Benz – he's managed to get completely pissed without even 'mussing', as they say in America, his hair. On his crazy drink-drive, the collar of his jacket is turned the wrong way round. That's *all*. He gets arrested, jerked around by the cops, and appears before the judge next morning and the suit and the shirt both look great. But this is the point in the picture where you start to worry about Cary's personal hygiene. Start to ITCH. Cops aren't generally too open-handed with showers.

It's back to the bad guy's house, then to the Plaza, looking good. I always hope he'll grab a quick shower in George Kaplan's hotel room – he keeps gravitating towards the bathroom. There's a good suit moment when he tries on one of the suits belonging to Kaplan, the guy he's looking for, who doesn't exist. *They're* stodgy, old-fashioned, unbelievably heavy for a summer in New York, with *cuffs on the trousers*. So much for US Government sartorial acumen. 'I don't think that one does anything for you,' says Cary's mom, and boy is she right. She also jokes that Kaplan maybe 'has his suits mended by invisible weavers', which *is* what happens to Cary's suit throughout the picture! His suit is like a victim of repeated *cartoon violence* – in the next shot it's always fine.

Off to the United Nations, where the Secretariat looks even more like Cary than his own office building did. He sublimely matches a number of modern wall coverings and stone walls here and throughout the picture. He pulls a knife *out* of a guy, but doesn't get any blood on himself. (There's a curious lack of blood in *North by Northwest*; it must be all to save the suit, though they must have had ten or even twenty of them, no?) He evades the bad guys again and scoots over to Grand Central Station, where they have, or had, showers, but he's too busy . . .

This is what's ingenious about this picture, at least as far as the SUIT goes – Cary's able to travel all over the country in just this one beautiful suit because the weather has been *planned for the suit by Ernest Lehman*! It's the perfect weather for an adventure in this suit, and that's why it happens. At the same time, there's a CREEPINESS about the whole escapade generated by your *own* fears that in some situation Cary will be inappropriately dressed (Cary GRANT?) and this will hinder him, or that the thin covering of civilisation the suit provides him will be pierced and here he's thousands of miles from home with not so much as a top coat. The fears one always has of being too cold in a suit (Glen Cove, Long Island, even on a summer night) or too hot (the prairie, to come). Exposed, *vulnerable*. He does have some money though, we know that, so he could buy something to wear if he had to, assuming his wallet hadn't been destroyed if the suit was. But it would be too traumatic to see this suit getting totalled, that would be way beyond Hitchcock's level of sadism. This feeling of exposure, the idea of having suddenly to make a desperate journey in just what you have on, comes up in *The Thirty-Nine Steps* (book and movie) where Richard Hannay is alone in a desolate landscape in inappropriate town clothes, an evil-looking 'autogiro' spotting him from the air . . .

In the suit are a number of subtle tools for Cary. It's so well cut you can't tell if he's even carrying a wallet (turns out he is). Here's what he's got in that suit! He goes all the way from New York to Chicago to the face of Mount Rushmore with: a monogrammed book of matches, his wallet and some nickels, a pencil stub, a hankie, a newspaper clipping, and his sunglasses, but these are shortly to be demolished when Eva Marie Saint folds him into the upper berth in her compartment. (Really this is a good thing, because Cary Grant in dark glasses looks appallingly GUILTY.) All this stuff fits *invisibly* into the pockets of the most wonderful suit in the world. Does the suit get crushed in the upper berth, even though his Ray-Bans are smashed? No. Cary keeps his jacket on in the make-out scene that follows. The suit defines him, he's not going to take off that jacket. I know this feeling.

When Cary and Eva Marie walk from the train into La Salle Street station the next morning, he's wearing a purloined red-cap's outfit, open at the neck and showing a triangle of snowy white undershirt, and she has the same white triangle peeping from under the jacket of her dark suit, which rather matched James Mason's the night before. But here are two little white triangles who spent the night together on the train. There might be an opportunity here in Chicago for a shower, you itch, but it looks like he chooses merely to loosen his shirt and have a quick shave, with Eva Marie's minuscule razor. His suit was temporarily stuffed into her luggage while he made his exit from the train in disguise. Has it suffered? Has it Hell, it looks like a million bucks, his shirt still blazes out. But now comes the suit's greatest trial, the crop-dusting scene at 'Prairie Stop'. This begins with a suit moment when he and the farmer eye up each other's attire from across the hot highway. Cary gets covered in dust from giant trucks going by (a deliberate *attack on the suit*), sweats like a pig (or should, *we* do), has to throw himself into the dirt, gets sprayed with DDT, then practically gets run over by a tanker, grappling with its greasy undercarriage and writhing around on the asphalt.

After all this and having fled the scene in a stolen pick-up truck, Cary has only his hankie with which to make himself presentable at the Chicago hotel where he thinks 'Kaplan' is staying. Still, he's done a pretty good job with it – he looks like he's been teaching school all afternoon – just a bit chalky. His tie is still pressed and the shirt is white, even the collar and cuffs. You cannot violate the white shirt of the 1960s. You might kill me but you will never kill this shirt.

By the way, Eva Marie enters this scene in a really luxurious red and black dress – a sign of her decadent double life with James Mason – and it's all pretty uncomfortable because now Cary is dirty, a DIRTY MAN loose in civilisation, too easily spotted . . . But the *suit* gets rescued here! Eva Marie tells Cary she'll have dinner with him if he'll let the valet clean it! Cary tells her that when he was a kid he wouldn't let his mother undress him. Eva Marie says, 'you're a big boy now' – in one sense Cary's growing up, from an impressive but essentially childish New York executive and, you suppose, a playboy, into a man taking charge of sorting his life out. He *grows into his suit* over the course of the adventure and finds a life (and wife) to suit him. In another sense, though, he maybe has a BONER – he's been sniffing round Eva Marie and suggesting a skirmish. This is all very good neurotic 1950s movie dialogue. I don't know who suffered more, who was the more repressed, the writer, the actors or the audience in those days.

So Cary takes off the suit, goes into the shower, she gives it to the valet, and she splits! The suit is not there, so Cary is not there. We get to see that he wears *yellow boxers*, another sign that he's a daring guy in a 'creative' profession – whew! (In the shower he doesn't do any Godzilla monstering, he *whistles*. Long time ago, huh?)

Once Cary gets to the auction gallery, the suit is *perfectly restored*, that valet is some little 'sponger and presser'. He gets in a fist fight (no blood), is arrested, taken to the airport, put on a plane to Rapid City . . . The next day it's hot as blazes at Mount Rushmore, but the shirt is clean, the suit's fantastically smooth, a hot breeze rustles it a little. The monument itself is wearing a rock-like suit in solidarity with Cary. He's turning into a rock, too (ignore what I said up there). Eva Marie arrives in mourning, essentially – black and dove grey; she's about to have to leave Cary and her entire life behind. James Mason is in a weird English fop get-up, to suggest I guess he's never been one of us, he's not long for these shores now. He's *frail*. Eva Marie 'shoots' Cary: no blood again, of course, as it's a charade, but wouldn't you think the CIA would have some *fake blood*? How else are they going to put this over on James Mason? He's not an idiot. But you can't do this to the suit.

Now the suit is in the woods for the 'reconciliation' scene with Eva Marie. This suit doesn't look too bad in the woods, and you reflect that Mount Rushmore seems a very *formal* national park, there were a lot of people dressed up in the cafeteria, paying their respects . . . Cary gets punched out for trying to interfere between the Professor and Eva Marie, AND WHEN HE WAKES UP

THE SUIT HAS BEEN CONFISCATED! The Professor has locked him in a hospital room with only a TOWEL to wear! He's not going anywhere! (Although you feel a lot of relief that he's had his second shower of the picture.) This then is the real act of betrayal: the Professor brings CARY GRANT a set of *hideous* clothes from some awful 'menswear shop' in Rapid City, you can just imagine the smell of it, Ban-Lon shirts and cheap belts: he gives him an *off-white* white shirt, a pair of black trousers, white socks and icky black *slip-ons*.

You get the creeps because this whole thing is about insecurity, exposure, *clothing anxiety*. When Cary escapes out to the window ledge he's inching his way along in a pair of *brand-new slip-ons which may not fit*! Your feet and hands start to sweat at this moment and they don't stop. But something major has occurred: *Cary is now in black and white*: everything is CLEAR to him, and he can act decisively OUTSIDE the suit, in order to be able to win it back. It's all wonderfully Arthurian. Now he knows 'what to do'. And for us there's the thrill of a badly-dressed Cary: the situation is now a real emergency.

Now he crawls off the hospital lintels and up the stone wall of James Mason's millionaire's hideaway, which looks so like the face of the office building in the beginning, the rectangles of a snazzy suit. And in this white shirt with no jacket, Cary is a sitting duck in the bright moonlight! *A New Yorker without a jacket on*. It is too frightening.

Delightful though, to discover that in the end, when Cary and Eva Marie are on the train back to New York (she in virginal white nightie), he's got his suit back! He's not wearing the jacket (woo-hoo!) but those are definitely the suit's trousers and his original shoes and the gorgeous socks. The shirt has remained impeccable. Like Arthur, he needs a woman to be safe, to be alive and to be a king, even on Madison Avenue. Now he really knows how to wear that suit.

I managed to acquire a pair of trousers several years ago that were somewhat like Cary's. They weren't tailor-made, and weren't the same quality of material of course, but the colour was really close and the hang of them wasn't bad. And they turned out to be Lucky trousers, very very Lucky. Until I burned a hole in them. The veneer of civilisation is thin, fellas. Exceeding thin.

My Beautiful Guy Hell

If women knew how we really thought about them,
they would never stop slapping us.

LARRY MILLER

As Sinclair Lewis and others have demonstrated, one of the biggest problems with America is men. They're a problem everywhere, but here only more so. Babbitt blundering around his bathroom, the soap-blinded belligerence of the United States towards the rest of humanity would be comic if this were not a nuclear age. Jocks, nerds, Army men, academics, senators – screw 'em. They simply will not face up to their responsibilities.

Godzilla

For a short time I lived in a hot little place in the great Central Valley of California. I'm sorry to keep bringing up California. I'm trying to focus on its pan-American aspects . . . I'd never try to assert that L.A. or San Francisco think the way the rest of the country does, even though there used to be an expression that 'California is the sea coast of Iowa', which meant that it was filled with staid, lower-middle-class types who went there during the Depression, and not guys with long beards who roller-skate to the ashram every day.

You might say this is an ultra male town; it could get an *award* for this. The economy is beer-based: most of the money generated is from selling beer to farmers and students (there's a branch of the state university). The rest of the economy is in beer-related retail enterprises: video shops, taco shops, gun shops, burger shops, T-shirt shops. There are a few nail salons because stale, beery men do attract *some* women; they seem a kind of service industry to the service industry.

So the place was full of jocks. Some of them were just jocks, some were studying to be jocks, some had flunked out but were jocks still. When the farmers came into town for their beer, they dressed and acted like jocks. Jocks congregated for some reason behind my apartment building on a Friday afternoon, to get their beer drinking going in the alley. Jocks have these *voices*, the kind of insistent, hollow, insecure voice that is bound to keep you awake at night. From a distance it sounds like all jocks mostly say is 'My mom my mom my mom my mom . . .' Occasionally something strident about pointless exercise breaks through this matriarchal rhubarb: 'DIRK can do a hundred miles easy. DIRK has no problem, MAN.' Have you ever had to listen to the name DIRK repeatedly emphasised in the middle of the night?

One night very late a great baritone jock was complaining about the tedious weekend cycle of hanging out and then having sex with random girls: 'Every Friday night it's the same thing, Burger King, motel room, Burger King, motel room.' He sounded really tortured about it. Good!

But there is one place where all men are jocks, are all in the Army, are all babies, and that is in the shower. (Don't get excited.) Come with me into the showers . . . don't be afraid . . . Let us admit to this: even if we are mannerly men, and most of us aren't, when no one is near, OR when we are surrounded, *threatened* by naked, vulnerable strangers, we ROAR. We grunt, sigh, hiss, fart, scratch our balls – either before or after pointless exercise, when the blessed (and, in American showers, *buffeting*) stream of water plays across our shoulders and chest, we ROAR, AGAIN and AGAIN, as if it's TORTURE instead of something pleasant, hygienic – whether we have come from the playing field or the inertness of the office, we ROAR, we scream and howl as if in ecstasy or open-heart surgery.

You know how amazed, how *pained* Godzilla acts when they shoot at him with their puny howitzers, when they buzz him with their gnat-like fighter planes? Godzilla is merely a man in a stream of hot water, that's where they got the idea – the way he roars, claws at the air, at nothing. This torrent somehow releases the cellular memory of every ill, every injury or slight, every desire: we claw the air and BELLOW, rocking from side to side. We're so bloody unhappy it's just not funny, MAN. It's a big problem for DIRK, MAN. Uggh! Agggggh! In the past, if there ever was one, anyone'd have called the police if they heard the kind of noises modern man makes in the shower.

Just what is *so horrific* about your life, buddy? It sounds like you're being disembowelled. But that's how men 'feel' every day. Life is *killing* them. And nobody understands. Agggg-Ahhhhhh! AGGH! Look at this guy, he's standing with his arms and legs spread, like he's been *ordered* to, he's hanging off the curtain rail, twisting himself under the spray like it's a 6,000°F beam of superheated shit straight from Hell! AAAAAAGGGHHH! He loves it. In the next shower is the guy I call Sudzilla: moaning and yelling he works himself up into a total masculine *soap frenzy* . . . You never get a good look at Sudzilla, how can you?, but from his cubicle comes pile after pile of huge fluffy suds – soap and shampoo and maybe even some kind of schmancy 'body wash' all at the same time, and who knows what else? Maybe Sudzy's cleaning out the old *vas deferens* at the same time, it all depends on what my mom my mom my mom told him about his rights in the shower . . .

Now get this one: he *lumbers in*, malevolently – whether into the shower, the sauna, the weight room, and whatever he's doing, working out or sweating it out, even in the shower he SQUATS, all the time he's squatting and ROARING. (I've seen him outside, he wears a suit – not surprising really, but I mean apparently he has a JOB.) OK let's get the Hell out of here, we walk back to our LOCKERS, again how infantile can you get, why do men insist on remaining at school their whole lives?, *lockers* . . . Right here there's a naked guy glaring at himself in the mirror, he's making the Godzilla gestures, tearing frantically at his hair. What he's trying to do is to get his crew cut to *stand up* with the wax he's put on it, pawing his own head with enough force to scalp himself: 'God DAMN it, God DAMN it!' he yells. Also here we have to carefully walk around a guy, the TRAINER, *Narcizilla*, who walks up and down in front of the mirrors before a work-out, gazing at his own muscles. He does this longer than the sessions take. I've timed him.

Girls, male weight-training and body-building are just another way of being fat. By dint of hard work you turn yourself into a blobby pink triangle or cone with a fuel hole at the top. Look at what these bastards EAT! What about the rest of us?

The bravest, most muscle-zilla thing a man can do is STALK AWAY ROARING from all his wet towels on the floor. Your mom your mom your mom . . . going to get the better of her yet!

There's a man of twenty-five who yells 'FUCK! FUCK!! FUCK!!!' outside my house at three thirty every morning.

A close friend of mine who grew up in an adoptive family spent a number of years looking for his natural father and finally found him. At their first meeting, the father sort of aggressively sized him up, and grasping his own crotch, said, 'You wanna compare sizes?' Men are a happy bunch. I'm telling you girls, there's no end to it.

My Little Cabinet

Being a collector of sorts, a NERD!!, whose chest of Interesting (Purchased) Rocks disappeared in some move years ago, whose interest in book collecting was demolished by working in the rare book trade, and whose minor gathering of *petits Tours Eiffels*, Empire States and plaster Colossea is only mocked, MOCKED I tell you, I have begun a little Cabinet of Egomaniacs, all of whom, so far, are male.

My prize exhibit is a guy, a fascinating, unbearable guy of about sixty, who came into the bar a few months ago, trailing a truly beleaguered-looking wife and a young man who might have been a nephew, or an acolyte in the same field, which might have been history, or easily zoology. He walked all around the place, admiring the woodwork, pointing out various decorative bits of decorative rubbish from 1920 . . . 'Marvellous!' he crowed, 'what a magnificent bar it is, *no?*' to his companions, who obviously didn't give a damn about bars or their various stupid appurtenances. He had such long floppy grey hair and PEERED at us all *over the tops of his spectacles*, and worked his jowly mouth like a fish, when he wasn't pontificating or monopolising the conversation.

My wife has little patience for the infinite varieties of male ridiculousness at the best of times. Time-wasting attention-seekers in particular make her BLAST OFF. I asked what she thought this guy's name was, and her immediate answer was, 'Hugh Grating-Loss.' And yes, that *had* to be his name; we could immediately picture him at home, sitting all day in a hideous damp armchair in England, smoking endless cigarettes and drinking cups of coffee stretching to infinity, hectoring, lecturing, brushing *crumbs of food* off himself when visitors came to *pay homage*. He was one of those men who tells everybody either what they already know, or don't care to know, in an EXTREMELY LOUD voice.

The wife and acolyte had no interest in Scotch (which has been nerdised to the point of intolerability), and somehow even he perceived this. So he started practically YELLING THE HISTORY OF SCOTCH into the cringeing, abashed face of the only other guy at the bar, a mild man who, despite looking like a tramp, is in fact of a ducal family and knows more about the real history of Scotch than anyone else in this town. He nodded with a kind of squashed, sheepish, blinky surprise at each Erroneous Pronouncement of Hugh Grating-Loss.

THEN, Hugh ordered a *Glenlivet*, so much for taste and interest. He fish-moued and gaped and blinked as if there was some mystical value accruing to him for his being there and being 'in the know'. We had to leave, but if I could I would have followed him around for days.

Men and Knives

In the 1950s men waded into the kitchen and nerdised it. My own father possessed a barbecue apron which had a picture of a Happy Dad grilling meats on it and the slogan IT'S A MAN'S WORLD.

It was printed in dark blue and red, very MEATY, and as it faded over the years the colours started to look like bad meat. But my father was never a man to believe things written on aprons.

Chefs. Anthony Bourdain admits to using twenty rolls of paper towels in a day. They all go on and on about their *knives* (impotence – scary). Their creepy catalogue of mostly *Germanic*-sounding equipment which could have come straight out of an arms-trading fair: *Gaggenau, Bulthaup, Wüsthof Dreizac, Gutmann, Rutt* . . . How 'bout the Oppenheimer World-Oven? Let's all get in. They're all in denial about even having food around, hiding it in minimalist-fantasist cabinets and icky looking morgue-style cold drawers . . . What did their parents *do* to these guys? Almost all of them are 'separated from' their wives, though one supposes not far enough.

If you want to know something of a humbler United States – just for a kind of bleak fun – chase up an old copy of *The Joy of Cooking* by Irma Rombauer. There you will find recipes for wholesome food (albeit sometimes too dependent on things tinned – there had recently been a war on) which cost about 25¢ a time. Food which seems as nice and antique as the ¢ sign itself. Looking at Irma's book you get a sense of scale, of humility, of . . . *happiness* long gone, compared to the icky feelings about your fellow man, the sense of shame, even panic you get in perusing a magazine like *Food and Wine*. Food, like everything else, will barely exist in the coming nerdy reality. It will be only photographs and longings.

Rick Stein had his collection of knives confiscated at the

airport in Cleveland once. What did he expect? But poor chefs, losing their weaponry, being *feminised* by the Age of Terrorism. I bet *Irma Rombauer* didn't run all over the place with a bunch of knives rolled up in a towel – *she* said all you need is a meat knife, a bread knife, a paring knife and (lovely Americanism) a grapefruit knife.

Internationally famous chef and boyish, shouting anal retentive Gordon Ramsay has said, talking of his *own home*, with its oven which cooks at 600 degrees centigrade: 'What do I want to have a dinner party here for? Everyone will be expecting fantastic food and the last thing I want to do is create at that level.'

Well, what's the oven for? Roasting his own nuts? And what 'level' were our fathers cooking 'at' in the back yard? Why did men steal the art of cooking and turn it into the Manhattan Project?

I have stopped feeling sympathetic to any apologists for war, especially Robert Oppenheimer and the other NERDS who got us into the nuclear fix we are in, which we are only going to get out of, in the end, by 'mutual assured destruction'. I stopped being interested in *Robert Oppenheimer's conscience* a long time ago – these technological men who 'just couldn't help themselves' making thermonuclear weapons because of the motherfucking (literally) 'spirit of scientific enquiry'. Guys like this also 'just can't help themselves' raping ten-year-olds. Oppenheimer felt bad about what he did? I bet he doesn't feel as bad about it as we do. I'm willing to bet he feels nothing.

All the Usual Boy's Room Stuff

Before you have any grasp on what's really interesting (WOMEN), you get, or are given, these nerdy ideas about what is interesting. *Crepuscular inklings* of what is of value in the world: there is an older kid on the block who has access to this stuff, so you end up hanging around him, even though you don't like him and your parents would FREAK if they knew anything about him or took a good look at him. Hell, when I was nine I spent time with one of the biggest idiots in southern California just because he had a ten-room tree house and a pet monkey. Which filled the tree house with monkey shit.

Our guy, K's and mine, was BJ. If this sounds unlike us, I can only offer that this was about a year before Thoreau hit. A schematic of BJ's bedroom, which was a kind of semi-adult pleasure palace – if he could have got away with it he'd have been serving beer: the walls were covered with enamel soft drink signs, stolen road signs, disturbing electric clocks showing polarised waterfalls advertising Hamm's beer, *Playboy* calendars, satin banners proclaiming automotive products. What is it with *CAR* guys and *cheap satin*? Their idea of luxury chills you to the bone.

Attaching yourself to beer, products, printed representations of tits seemed a real thrill at the time. But today everyone's a walking billboard for stuff they know from nothing, so what am I screaming about?

The hidden meaning of all this *worship of appurtenances* may be a hope that they will *propel* you into adulthood, therefore into the arms of women, but lots of men, being nerds, get stuck right here. They worship a brand of spark plug for the rest of their lives, before they can even know a spark plug to move a CAR towards their date, towards HAPPINESS. They can't really face the happiness. Lots of men, boys, just worship that ol' spark plug on its banner, they've lost track of women, they lose themselves in that ol' polarised waterfall of BEER before they even get started – the beer that's being drunk by all the other guys in the pine-panelled bar who've *already failed with women*, rightly been kicked out by them. Pretending, always pretending that it doesn't matter. As men, our lives are over before they've begun, HELP.

But what were we to know? BJ's stuff seemed to be about a life that was to come, not the little death of men. We sat there in astonishment, and here was BJ telling me in all seriousness, when I'd ogled his circular yellow railroad crossing sign: 'Well, the best way to start a sign collection is by stealing one of these NO PARKING TODAY signs.' They were temporary, cheap apparently, never very strongly affixed to lamp posts by our over-conscientious municipality. These signs had the same evanescent meaning as BJ's moustache, the only one strong enough to register in the 9th grade yearbook photographs, though in the world of hair it was not one of the killer organisms.

Other stuff of BJ's – a yellow badge showing long fingers, chopsticks, a rice bowl: YELLOW POWER. This was a joke on 'black power'. Ha. I hadn't figured out yet the politically toilet-bound nature of this kind of stuff, the politics of this kind of bedroom. I wanted it! As if we were buying a lid or something we made a deal there in the flickering commercial lights of BJ's bedroom, a deal for two of the satin banners advertising CASTROL, which he would get for us *mint in box* from some shadowy source. K and I rode our bikes home in the dark. Once we were out of the lurid confines of BJ's room, I wasn't sure we had concluded a transaction of value. K looked thoughtful. 'No, it seems good,' he said, 'they're only eight dollars – where else are we going to get them, all clean, for that much money?' This was inarguable; I wasn't into the theft side of this hobby, or 'life style' – what was I going to do if I really needed one of these banners, run into a garage full of *mechanics* and swipe one of these things in broad daylight? But why did we *need* these? What was CASTROL anyway? What we primarily admired about BJ was the ease with which he acquired *Playboy* magazines, all *Playboy* products.

Summary judgement of the man who ran the grocery store on California Street when, with real panache and indifference, K and I each plunked down in front of him identical piles of purchases consisting of a copy of *Playboy* underneath three packages of notebook paper and a jar of baby food (this on the advice of BJ: 'buy baby food with your *Playboy*, he'll think you're married'):

NOT FOR YOU, KID!

We got our CASTROL promotional banners, mint in box as promised, and K even put a down payment with BJ for a big illuminated Pepsi clock – here K was a lot cooler and smarter than I was, he was really going to get the BJ bedroom. My father seemed pretty sceptical of my BANNER, when he spotted it on my wall. 'I hope you're not going in for CAR stuff,' he said, 'there's no future in that.'

Although he had an actual *work bench* and a *tool chest* in the garage, he and I had but a slim relationship to real GARAGE MALES, i.e. we had some nifty-looking matching screwdrivers in a BOX, a number of rather pretty old-fashioned planes and augers that had belonged to Grandfather, but these were for working in WOOD for god's sake, whereas the Other Dads, the real GARAGE MALES on our block had metal-lathes, HOISTS, bar-folders, chassis punches and timing-lights, because they worked on motors, CARS, amateur radio – they were *garage males*.

We were not garage male, but fortunately for our reputation as a family we were related to a guy who was alpha-garage-male, had it in buckets: Harry, my mother's 'shirt-tail' cousin, which in America is what you call someone when you are actually related to them by blood but don't want to be. It is a useful expression.

Harry really was a mechanic (aeroplanes) by profession, but when he wasn't at work he was in his garage, in which he had dedicated his *entire life* to restoring a very ancient CAR. The 'restoration' involved making the thing from scratch, as when he bought the CAR it was really only a rusty frame. Harry taught himself everything he needed to know to do this, even upholstery. As in our house, Harry's garage was right off the kitchen, he could dash indoors and eat a sandwich and rush back to the CAR – he did this for *thirty years*, I kid you not, years longer than the CAR had been derelict. Instead of berating him, or feeling slighted, in their state of extreme exasperation his wife and son also talked only of the CAR.

On his rare visits to our house (three streets from his own) Harry sat on the family sofa in confusion, looking hurriedly washed and brushed up, a little like Dagwood Bumstead. I made him nervous because I couldn't talk about football. He grinned at me: 'I guess you have your own room.' I said I did. 'That's a great thing, to have your own room. Guess you have, what, all the usual boy's room stuff in there, huh?' This question stopped me dead. Yeah, I guess so, I said. I didn't know if Harry wanted to see my room, to *get himself off the sofa*, or maybe he thought there would be something mechanical in there, some kind of CAR.

The usual boy's room stuff huh . . . I experienced a worrying flash of BJ's room – what would happen if Harry found himself somewhere like that? What *did* I have in my room? I thought. I had my 'Castrol' banner, which I was sure Harry would approve, he might even be able to tell me what 'Castrol' *was*. I had an old clock from the Western Union telegraph company, which didn't work but looked neat-o. The remains of an HO-gauge model railroad which was never going to go anywhere since I had conceived the idea of laying the track free-hand, the last of my involvements with the mechanical world. I was embarrassed to be the proprietor of a room decorated with Cowboy Wallpaper, which I had not requested and decidedly didn't want and was still STUCK with. I was furious that my mother and father had overlooked my violent aversion to cowboys and everything Western, even when I was seven, which was when they rushed in and glued it up one day over my *screams*. But this wallpaper would, I supposed, qualify as *all the usual boy's room stuff*. There was also my snare drum, resting at a jaunty angle on its stand, my Ludwig 002 sticks balanced neatly on the head. So: boy. Room.

But if I had been obliged to show Harry around my room, in all conscience as an honest male talking to a garage male, his eyes would have come to rest on my very complicated tool box with many drawers, which used to have all the railroad stuff in it but was now filled with the materials of my new hobby, that of theatrical and MONSTER make-up. You see, I was very unhappy in myself and my appearance, despite playing my DRUM, so this seemed perfect, to make yourself look like anything else, Chinese, African, female, or give yourself a gaping wound with eyeball dangling out, really express what you thought your prospects in the world were – !

So these are the things I'm happiest with, Harry, these twenty shades of Max Factor pancake, this liquid latex, this thing I made out of a coat hanger to stretch my mouth open abominably like Lon Chaney. And my prize possession at the moment Harry is this ten-ounce, fifteen-dollar tin of 'Naturo Plasto' MORTICIAN'S WAX, yes it's the real thing used by the best embalmers and when you heat it on the stove it makes your lovely Mom actually puke.

Nah.

And then, possibly stumbling backwards away from me, no, *no*, he'd see the small heavy chest Grandfather had given me, which used to hold radio equipment in the Army. In this chest were the instruments of my state, the illicit things you need to have at this budding stage of your nerdhood. What the chest contained was explosives: a number of neatly stacked packets of firecrackers Grandfather had sneaked into my room last Hallowe'en, firecrackers from Chinatown with labels so beautiful I could barely bring myself to set light to them, AND a number of neatly stacked copies of *Playboy*, all K and I had been able to garner from BJ and other more obscure sources, obviously not the grocery store. Neatly stacked . . . As a friend of mine who makes a speciality of staying in other people's houses said once, 'Everybody has contraband'. In safeguarding something we would be condemned for, we men somehow safeguard ourselves. We're idiotic.

All men are nerds, and that is a very bad thing, not a little thing, and this is the how of it: they're cowards, insensitive and greedy. They want *stimulus* all the time, violence, sex, meat, noise. But since you can't get any of these things all the time, men register them mentally as fetishes, as *statistics*. So when there is no football to be played or gaped at, there are the statistics. When there is no way of conveying the sublime, in listening to Haydn, there are the stats – this is how men deal with art. They make a list of the 'hundred best books of all time' and then beat your ass with it.

This is the way they wage war now, making it into a computer game, the endless *stats* of the deaths of civilians.

The problem with men (= nerds) is that they *replace* the meaning, the *joy* of something (Haydn, food, sex) with an icon of it, a sketch, something that can be LOGGED ON TO in the absence of the thing itself in your life; when the thing becomes too real or annoying or too hard for ittle man to understand. So instead of Haydn you have radio announcers telling you what to think the exciting part of this Haydn quartet is; instead of sex you get empty corsets.

What you have is – nothing, really. No way to experience anything that is real. And this male reality empty of reality makes these guys as mad as Godzilla. There is a vast conspiracy aiming at making sure that *nothing* will be real at all, eventually. What are computers but little machines that pre-nerdise reality for men? Now we are all sitting in front of these screens . . . This languor, this laxness will be used to a sinister purpose once the next attractive Hitler comes along. We already have the funnels jammed into our mouths.

Soon to be a Major Motion Picture

For American civilisation to reach an apotheosis, or even a flowering comparable to that of the nineteenth century, it would have been necessary for the motion picture, the quintessential American art, to be universally adaptable. Since the book is dying and film triumphant, America could have surpassed itself by realising a dynamic in which books previously thought to be unfilmable were made filmable.

The Wealth of Nations 1938 dir. Ernst Lubitsch. Leslie Howard, Edward Arnold. *In 1780 London, a bewigged coffee-house bore tells everyone what to do.*

Das Kapital 1950 dir. Erich von Stroheim. Ernest Borgnine, Robert Coote (as Engels). *In 1890 London, an enormous German terrorises the Establishment with his boils.*

Hiawatha 1955 dir. John Ford. Jack Palance, Marlene Dietrich. *A man of Chippewa descent is driven mad by rhythmic pounding.*

Jubilate Agno 1949 dir. Lewis Milestone. Danny Kaye, Cyd Charisse. Jeoffry the Cat: Bert Lahr. *A kooky poet is obsessed with making lists.*

The Prelude 1940 dir. Jean Renoir. David Niven, Margaret Lockwood. *Failing to think only of his sister, a North of England man steals a boat and goes to college.*

The Raw and the Cooked 1960 dir. Howard Hawks. John Wayne, Sidney Poitier. *On safari, a white hunter realises he does not understand the significance of dinner.*

Theory of the Leisure Class 1955 dir. Billy Wilder. Sammy Davis Jr, Frank Sinatra, Peter Lawford, Joey Bishop, Angie Dickinson. *Four philosophers visit Las Vegas and learn how to relax.*

The Double Helix 1962 dir. Roger Corman. Dean Jones, Wally Cox, Sandra Dee, Whit Bissell. *Two wacky bachelors invade a lab and try to cook up the perfect wife.*

The Origin of Species 1960 dir. George Cukor. Rex Harrison, Trevor Howard, Sabu. *A bored aristocrat sails to the South Seas, where he tells animals what to do.*

Revolution and the State 1931 dir. King Vidor. Charles Middleton, Joan Blondell. *A diminutive Russian has plans to dominate the earth but is filled with embalming fluid instead.*

Francis – SPQR (aka *'The Golden Ass'*) 1955 dir. Fred de Cordova. Sterling Holloway, Donald O'Connor, Francis the Talking Mule. *Fiddling around in ancient Rome, Francis engages the Senate in boisterous toga play.*

The Cantos 1947 dir. Douglas Sirk. Adolphe Menjou, Linda Darnell. *A caged poet dreams of better days.*

Six Crises 1962 dir. Raoul Walsh. Dwayne Hickman, Jane Wyman. *A jobless loner tells his peasant father of his decision to run for President.*

Mastering the Art of French Cooking 1960 dir. Jean-Luc Godard. Jayne Mansfield, Jean-Paul Belmondo. *In occupied France, a dizzy WAC discovers a sauce that fights Nazism.*

Baby and Child Care 1968 dir. Russ Meyer. Leo G Carroll, Jerry Mathers, Patty Duke, Jay North, Oliver North. *A mad doctor finds he has reared a nation of narcissistic monsters.*

Civilisation and its Discontents 1940 dir. Rene Clair. Fred MacMurray, Greta Garbo, Robert Benchley (as Jung). *A timid European doctor is haunted by his own penis.*

See also the musical sequel:

Vienna Holiday 1950 dir. Victor Fleming. William Powell, Sonja Henie. *After a scary dream, Dr Freud falls in love with a pretty skater.*

Brandenburg Concerto 1945 dir. William Wellman. Sydney Greenstreet, Zsa Zsa Gabor. *A beautiful countess befriends a morose wurst-eater and inspires him to musical greatness.*

Paradise Lost 1947 TECHNICOLOR dir. Alfred Hitchcock. Don Ameche, Loretta Young. *In Yellowstone National Park, a blind, psychotic forest ranger frames a newlywed couple for littering.*

The I Ching 1955 dir. James Wong Howe. Myrna Loy, Sidney Toler, Keye Luke. *Charlie Chan tracks a mysterious girl gambler who never seems to lose.*

The Embarrassment of Riches 1995 dir. Joel and Ethan Coen. Matt Damon, Scarlett Johansson, Kate Winslet. *In 1650 a nation of tiny cheese eaters launches an attack on the island of Bali with chocolate cannonballs.*

Seven Types of Ambiguity 1965 dir. John Ford, Jean-Luc Godard, Woody Allen, John Cassavetes, Russ Meyer, Roman Polanski, Cecil B. De Mille. Bob Hope, Anna

Magnani, James Mason, Judy Garland. *Four wacky intellectual castaways keep warm by knitting amazing neck beards.*

Germs 2005 dir. Mike Leigh. Jack Nicholson, Nicole Kidman, Danny De Vito (as Kurt Weill). *Frightened by a newspaper, a frail young art historian gets an erection.*

Wittgenstein's Nephew 1998 dir. Michael Crichton. Matt Damon, Arnold Schwarzenegger. *Two wacky invalids discuss philosophy and get wheeled around a hospital.*

Woodcutters 1997 dir. Baz Luhrmann. Jim Carrey, Hy Anzell, Anna Nicole Smith. *At a cocktail party in 1970 Vienna, a man longs for a newspaper, he thinks, sitting in the wing chair.*

Time to Get into Jambos

On Saturday mornings my sister and I would rise about five thirty to get started on watching television all day. We got our own breakfasts, always cold cereal, *the cold cereal of the moment*. She usually went for SUGAR POPS, while my favourite was KIX, whatever they may be. I retain the name, but no memory of what they looked or tasted like. The family's octagonal brown and white sugar bowl was, in fact, sacrosanct, but as 'nobody' was UP . . . I can't stomach cold cereal now, I'd be just as happy, if not happier, to eat the BOX. But we certainly shovelled it down, bowl after bowl, in the bluish-white slurry of milk and pounds of sugar, in the bluish-white rays of the TV. *Until*, about eleven or so, our father appeared and, appalled by the sight of the milk-churning distended bellies of his albino slug offspring in their sea cave, YANKED the drapes open in an attempt to force us out of doors, a very unkind thing to do to photophobic, hypoglycaemic slowworms. Someone oughta call the SPCA. This was always a horrific shock to the system and sent us into an immediate quarrelsome rage against each other, even though we'd got along fine until *he* arrived. Under duress I would put on my clothes and go out. After several years of listless neighbourhood play I realised I could go get a friend and bring him back to our house to watch the Monster Movies which started at 1.30 p.m. – by that time my father would be involved in one of his plumbing and swearing projects. So by the age of ten I watched ten hours of TV on a Saturday.

Saturday was not the best day to find anyone to play with, but now no one seeks to play in neighbourhoods. Children are individually driven in huge, heavily armoured vehicles to some kind of fortressed and/or electronic 'fun'.

It is too bad that you have to grow up and start wearing clothes, when practically everything good happens to you when you are little and in your JAMBOS. Wearing your jambos is like wearing your family and home, putting them on and buttoning them all around you; these warming, intangible securities. Ah, lying on the carpet watching TV in your jambos! (unless you had *very hard nylon carpeting*). We communed spiritually with the nation of kiddos in jambos, beyond bedtime, beyond our roof. Sometimes we were taken in the car IN JAMBOS to see fireworks on summer nights, once even allowed on the *roof of the car* so as to see better (again, unbearably wonderful) in my jambos and bathrobe and slippers. The clarion call: *TIME TO GET INTO JAMBOS!*, wherever you were, even at the home of some other family . . . it might mean hot chocolate, popcorn . . . *home movies!* When you are a kid, *home movies* don't signify excruciating boredom, they mean COSINESS.

My winter jambos were nice. My summer jambos were not

– of scratchy white nylon, they made me feel as if I should be examining someone's teeth. They had *snaps* – who invented *these* goddamn things? – snaps may be the most depressing thing to find on any garment. I was particularly aware of the scratching as I lay in bed listening to my parents having parties in the back yard in midsummer light, though it was past my bedtime, à la Robert Louis Stevenson. But *winter* jambos meant special moments. Weekend morning PANCAKES, the pancakes invariably made by American Fathers. The American Father makes these pancakes so that his children will always remember *this* breakfast, and *him*, and never the five thousand six hundred and sixteen other breakfasts given them by the American Mother until they graduate from high school. And CHRISTMAS, a holiday celebrated in some parts of America almost *entirely* in jambos, the kiddos, the parents, and even the grandparents in weird jambos from the late nineteenth and early twentieth centuries and purchased in a musty shop in a place you had never heard of. I always admired my Dad's deep-coloured tartan bathrobe and his slippers of wine-coloured levant leather, just enough worn to remind us of his very distant French heritage. To judge from paintings it would seem that in France all of life is conducted in slippers and some kind of derivative Turkish jambos, at least until the modern era, and even then – . Aren't *jambos* behind all of Flaubert?

In those days we had a large, comfortable, somewhat ornate sofa, upholstered in a faded rusty pink pattern. I was always happy on this sofa, as this is where my parents read to me. As with pyjamas, it is a bloody shame that you have to exchange the sofa for the world, or even go to bed; it still seems a shame.

Must we to bed, indeed? Well then,
Let us arise and go like men

STEVENSON

I don't think I was ever happy again, once having left the sofa more or less permanently, at least that is until I got MARRIED. Thirty years later. My mother read us AA Milne. She was an excellent actress and her impression of Eeyore is still beyond compare. My father specialised in Toad's voice in Kenneth Grahame, and read *The Wizard of Oz* and, stirringly to me, *Twenty Thousand Leagues Under the Sea*. These evenings were precious, because I was ON THE SOFA, and because they were accompanied with one snack or another, either RITZ crackers, a kind of nauseating greasy orange thing (from which, I'm not kidding, there was a way of making MOCK APPLE PIE, a frightening anachronism of the Depression), or POPCORN, which we were always given in small, bright-coloured aluminium bowls. I preferred the GREEN one. But more than these books I liked it best when Dad took out his guitar and sang to us. I liked the tortoiseshell finger rest on his Harmony guitar and the ivory-coloured pegs which held the strings in place. He sang 'Jimmy Crack Corn' if we were having popcorn, 'Go Tell Aunt Rhody' and 'When Johnny Comes Marching Home'. Music seemed to be a great thing, as comfortable and safe as JAMBOS, ornate and pillowed as the sofa, tasty as popcorn.

Drumming at the Edge of Parental Disapproval

At ten I got interested in the drums, not that I knew anything about them. I just liked the look of them. As has been usual in my life I could procure information *about* things I wanted (catalogue of the Ludwig Drum Company, Chicago, *Playboy* magazine, Chicago – hey! Is this why I married a girl from Chicago?), but not the things themselves. My only drum exemplars were Ringo Starr and Joe Morello – a kind of pan-democracy of the drums, I thought, on the one hand Ringo holding his sticks in louche unorthodox fashion in his jewelled fingers, smoking a cigarette in his black turtleneck. Then, a few pages over in *Ludwig Drummer* magazine, Joe Morello, who with his brush cut, horn rims and white shirt looked not so much a jazz exponent as a guy who worked for *IBM*.

So you have to start angling, talking about *the thing* all the time, showing your parents the depth of your current obsession until they get scared and take notice. It's one of the most exhausting chores of childhood. But I was hypnotised by the idea of drums.

I started making some out of potato crisp tins and layers of waxed paper, which I would play on with disposable wooden chopsticks (pathos) . . . When that failed to impress, I bought a little kid's metal drum, which at least had proper sticks. Nearly. Finally I trapped my mother in the kitchen (luckily for him, my father was away a lot at this time) and demanded at the very least the right to purchase a second-hand banjo (!) and saw the neck off (my kind of solution to the problem of the Unattainable Drum). This woke her to her impending ordeal, but, she said, to my surprise, that *were* we to acquire a drum, it would be a drum and not an *amputated banjo*. Which held me for a while.

The family was on the move in the early 1960s, along with the rest of the country. Once we got to our new place, 400 miles north, I began again my insistent tattoo of drum desire. What can it be like as a parent to realise that despite your best intentions THE DRUMS ARE COMING? How ever will you keep the drums from the door? I did get a drum, ONE DRUM – I never got to the SET, because drum sets are jazz, are rock, so – . Not in our family no sir.

And I got a drum teacher, *what* a cool guy. He had slicked-back hair, white Levis and black slip-ons. And a drum set. He later became a really well-known rock drummer, but in 1965 he was still in his 'greaser' phase. A good teacher, and a short walk from our house. Six months later, *somehow*, my parents discovered that he'd had a baby with a girl he wasn't married to, and I was obliged to tell him that I was no longer allowed to study with him. This was a real blow, as he was my only touchstone of cool.

I resented my father *accusing*, though not in person of course, my DRUM TEACHER of having, or 'committing' (his word) sexual intercourse, which I agreed was a very bad thing, practically unbelievable (though there was the baby). Sexual intercourse, I thought, is ruining my life.

The following week I found myself in a big Quonset hut on the other side of town, for what amounted, appropriately, to *military drumming instruction*. There was a kid from my class who drummed here, a frighteningly straight kid whose crew cut was just like his father's. It seemed to be mirrored in his rigidity and in the fine wirework of the braces on his teeth. We had actually to go out and drum in parades, in silly uniforms, from this place. There was a jazz teacher, with a drum set, up in the attic, but he looked pretty unlikely to be any avatar of cool, and anyway you weren't allowed to attend on him until you had passed your examination in the 'Rudiments', the *Gradus ad Parnassum* of snare drumming. The Rudiments (overseen by the National Association of Rudimental Drummers, a name so close to NERD that it hardly seems possible) gave me a bedrock sense of rhythm. I may not be much of a singer or a melody maker but I am a kind of weird human metronome, as anyone who's ever played with me will tell you. But despite this technical boon, here I was marching, literally marching away in the wrong direction as usual.

How I Killed Bluegrass

To Ken Salisbury

I have a very musical father. He was born in the middle of the woods, and by the time he was in high school he could play the piano, glockenspiel, guitar, 'sweet potato' and the trumpet. He can pick up any musical instrument and play it – within seconds he has figured the scale and is playing 'Over the Waves' or 'The Carnival of Venice'; it matters not if it is a koto, an oud or a theremin. He's probably playing 'Anchors Aweigh' on an ondes Martenot as I write this. When my sister and I were little he would play the guitar and sing to us: 'She'll Be Comin' 'Round the Mountain', 'Sweet Betsy From Pike', 'Frog Went A-Courting' – the standard-issue 1940s idea of 'folk songs', but he genuinely liked them, and so did we. It's nice to be sung to. He has a very good voice. Although I was not sure about 'She'll Be Comin' Round the Mountain'. I could never tell if it was about a horse, a train, or a lady.

To a small extent I inherited his abilities. I once made my friend Irving very angry by grabbing a saxophone he'd just paid a lot of money for and playing 'Over the Rainbow' on it. I don't know how I was able to do this, but it sure made him mad. He couldn't play a note.

I take up the banjo

For whatever reasons of parental paranoia, or perhaps just the parental need for QUIET, I was effectively forbidden from listening to or playing the popular music of my time. My parents would not stand for it. My sister had one Janis Joplin record which she hid under her bed, and listened to with headphones and a cigarette only when no one else was home. So I had to find something else. My friend Ken had acquired a used five-string banjo at a garage sale, and was in the habit of carrying it around with him, like the banjoist John Burke, in the hope that someone might show him how to play it. Then he found Pete Seeger's book *How to Play the Five-String Banjo* and started practising. I don't know why I was attracted to this, other than that there had been a rise in awareness of bluegrass, partly due to the inclusion of Flatt and Scruggs's 'Foggy Mountain Breakdown' in Arthur Penn's movie *Bonnie and Clyde*. We began to listen to that idiosyncratic piece of American music over and over again, the way boys do. The way *nerds* do. Because of the weird musical education we got at school, I tended to think of everything as 'programme' music, so at first I imagined that 'Foggy Mountain Breakdown' somehow *portrayed* an old car breaking down on a misty road in the Tennessee hills . . .

Music is a big racket in bourgeois places. Think of the numbers of factory violins, violas and clarinets in the world! Every schnook in our school wanted to play guitar, have a band, *wear a paisley shirt*. There were two men who had music shops in our town, and they preyed on us. I'm still afraid of them. One was an insinuating evil mercantile bastard, and the other just plain nuts, nuts enough to draw you in to his own screwiness – dreams of fame – great claims made for appalling, foreign-made instruments . . . Our friend Kris got some small revenge on the evil one by spotting a vintage Dobro slide guitar in his shop and paying only a few dollars for it – the old bastard had no idea what it was. He was too busy selling Bakelite saxophones and pasteboard drum sets to all these worried-looking zitty kids and their parents.

My father was reachable, tractable on the level of musical instruments, and so from one of these borderline personalities I acquired my first banjo, the shell of which really was plastic, made by the Harmony company. But it wasn't totally awful (my next one was worse), it had a plunky quality which suited the 'clawhammer', folky stuff I started playing. The main problem with crummy banjos is that the fingerboards aren't as wide as they should be. So there is only so far you can get in the quest for an Earl Scruggs pyrotechnic style. My first teacher had a beautiful vintage Epiphone banjo with a flashy 'tone ring' pressing up against the head. The action of the strings was much lower than on mine and I used to hunger after its wide, slightly curved fingerboard. When he played he sounded like Earl Scruggs. I was plunky.

For a long time the dominant hemisphere of my banjo brain was the folky one. This was mixed up with my growing environmental paranoia. I had developed my little personal ethos there with my old green copy of *Walden*, an olive-green knapsack I always had with me in which I put *Walden,* my old horse chestnut, my Mollenhauer tenor recorder (on which I played Seegerish, fipply nonsense when I went for one of my thousand lonely hikes), and always wearing Dunham hiking boots. If I dressed like Pete Seeger, if we *all* dressed like Pete Seeger, we would slow the conveyor-belt to material disaster we were all on. It now seems ridiculous to have thought that we could have deterred the mendacious way the world has gone just by playing acoustic musical instruments, in the light of what my generation has accomplished politically and environmentally, *which was to shirk our responsibilities while listening to Bob Dylan.*

As an adherent of 'Frog Went A-Courting', my father was annoyed and made ferocious by what he perceived as the *creeping socialism* of Seeger. I'd come out with 'The Banks are Made of Marble', or 'Joe Hill', or 'Guantanamera' and he'd look like he was going to throw up. 'Where does Pete Seeger get off singing about manual labour?' he said to me one day. 'Pete Seeger went to *Harvard.*' Well, how rude! *He* used to sing 'The Union Maid' to me on the sofa, with my RITZ crackers! But he did have a point.

The genius of Flatt and Scruggs

Earl Scruggs was the son of a banjo player, and came up with a unique way of playing it that is just as shrouded in mystery as the evolution of the five-string banjo itself. He joined Bill Monroe's band in 1945. It's hard to picture how bluegrass fit in to that post-war American world – what does it have to do with Dana Andrews and wide lapels, cigarettes, William Bendix going ape and bitter blondes? So far as I know it never appeared in any motion picture. It was way out there. Lester Flatt was already in the group. After two years they decided to leave Monroe, and founded the Foggy Mountain Boys. (Thus spawning a crippling tradition of the naming of bluegrass bands, employing excruciating synonym play: the Misty Mountain Boys, the Foggy Hill Boys, the Dank Plateau Boys, on and on. Several years ago there was a female bluegrass band I admired called the All Girl Boys.) Flatt and Scruggs had a great slide guitar player, Josh Graves, the bassist Jake Tulloch, and a genius of a fiddler named Paul Warren. They were a smash. They re-defined, solidified really, what bluegrass should sound like, and what it *meant*.

You have to forgive Americans for thinking their stuff is ancient. There *isn't* anything ancient in America, except the buried houses and bones of all the people we exterminated to achieve our big beautiful mess. I was a chump about bluegrass. I thought it must have existed for thousands of years. Something that *sounds pure*, we as a nation mistake for the gen-u-wine article. Bill Monroe invented the 'high lonesome' sound of bluegrass, although Lester Flatt and Earl Scruggs had almost everything to do with defining it. Let's be frank. Bluegrass is a depressed music, rooted in political ignorance, social dislocation, poverty, degraded religion, poor education and bad health. It's an artificial, commercial music, concocted only twenty years before I came across it. In time I found my way through the breakdowns, the broken-heart lyrics, 'My Cabin in Caroline', 'I'll Never Shed Another Tear', to the gospel numbers.

Despite my atheism, I did gravitate to these, recognised (if I didn't support) the sincerity of 'Take Me in the Lifeboat', 'Going to Heaven Sometime' and 'I Hear a Sweet Voice Calling'. Gospel music of whatever stamp is a vigorous American tradition, and it says something for a people making their worship the way they want it. Don't see no Europeans doin' that. The bluegrass gospel numbers are the most melodious, the four-part harmony shown off best, and the songs themselves perhaps the most touching. Bluegrass is an immense Kingdom of Bathos, full of dead or dying children. 'No Word from Home'. 'Don't Sell Daddy Any More Whiskey'. And for women it's a regular *Grand Guignol*. Poor Ellen Smith.

Recently I sat down to play some of these gospel tunes. But the bellicosity of American religionists and the behaviour of the Republican Party over the last few years made them seem monstrous. They sounded like advertisements for the Dark Ages. Religious people are tearing the world apart. Soon what I believe in will be gone and we will be left with only what *they* want. So I'm now opposed, yet again, to religion. I've lost the tender view

I had of the insides, the intricate, intimate beauties of the songs I had imagined plaintive. They STICK IN MY CRAW, MA.

I am the needle in the haystack. I am the bad egg, the cough in the carload. I am the turkey in the straw.

Interlude: Doc Watson

Was there ever a better, more sincere, more elegant American performer than Doc Watson? His voice was like the coldest rushing creek. When I discovered Doc Watson I assumed instantly that he had existed from the beginning of time and that he would always be there, sort of like Abraham Lincoln. In 1969 a few of us went to see him at a local college – to our amazement and delight he was not performing in an auditorium, but took a chair in one of the student lounges – there couldn't have been more than forty people there. I was about three feet from him, enraptured. He played his Martin guitar and sang so beautifully and *politely*, as was his way, for an hour. Then he felt his Braille watch, and smiled, and said it was time he was going. The *delicacy* of the man.

Battle in heaven between Earl Scruggs and Pete Seeger

The five-string banjo can be played in several different ways, and I wanted to master them all. Adolescents are always dazzled by virtuosity, and bluegrass seemed like it *might* acquire some rock-like status – Flatt and Scruggs had even performed at the Avalon Ballroom in San Francisco. *Man! That's the same place where the Dead and Moby Grape play!* So maybe some girls would admire that. And saving the planet and wearing jeans and flirting with the Reds – surely *some* girl would find that cool. At least *one*. Trying to figure out whether to throw in my lot with Scruggs or Seeger used to keep me awake at night. Ken was now leaning heavily towards Scruggs, though we had both started with Seeger. I worried that this could lead to a fistfight, which I could ill afford, as he was practically the only person at school who would have anything to do with me. But he was a real pragmatist and an easy-going guy, and I should have realised that he wouldn't have thought it necessary to choose sides. There was no denying Scruggs's musicianship. Seeger has always been canny about what virtuosity he has, so as to fake us out, or I should say to *include* all of us. Scruggs seemed truly modest about his achievement, a slow, steady craftsman's building of not only music but technique, lasting and beautiful. Seeger was always running around like a chicken with its head cut off, to use a barnyard analogy. Scruggs said that people always wanted him to be from Appalachia, which he wasn't; in a way you got the feeling that *Seeger* wanted to be from Appalachia, that he was some kind of neurotic *Harvard masochist*. There was something disturbing too about Seeger's pretension that he was somehow outside the commercial music business. He'd have liked you to think that he made his own records out the back, pressing them in a waffle iron. This made him look more nakedly ambitious than the Foggy Mountain Boys, driving easily around in their antiquated bus, sporting Kentucky colonel neckties. They sold these ties too, and we toyed with the idea of ordering some, but I think we decided we couldn't get away with this neckwear in the Summer of Love. Or any neckwear.

Ken and I both wrote fan letters to our idols. From Pete Seeger you got a very clever little piece of marketing – a little note with a sketch of one of his beloved Hudson river sloops at the top. It began 'Dear Friend, I'm glad you like my songs'. I was ecstatic for days until it dawned on me that it was only a form letter. From 'The Flatt and Scruggs Show' we received a short, hand-typed note on beautiful blue stationery, with a photograph of Lester and Earl looking vaguely heavenward, *from Mrs Earl Scruggs herself.* 'The Flatt and Scruggs Show' was a family business and radiated warmth and the homely intimations of their long-term sponsor, Martha White Self-Rising Flour. Whereas Mrs Seeger once said to Pete, 'I should write "pig" on the back of your shirt'!

The dilemma: what was roused in me by 'Foggy Mountain Breakdown'? Or by 'Living in the Country', part of Pete's arresting piece of genius, the *Goofing-Off Suite*? (This was a set of charming, literary-musical meditations that perfectly suited my growing ecological mania, buttressed with Thoreau and rolling up my sleeves.) I had to make a decision: Scruggs was the better musician and it was important to celebrate the classic things he had done for the banjo, elevating it to a dynamic, streamlined, inimitably American phenomenon (as if he were the Raymond Loewy of traditional music), and it was marvellous to dream of playing on stage with him, BUT if the America of 1968 erupted into open class and race warfare as we expected, I'd have to shoot him. The whole problem was settled, in a way, when Flatt and Scruggs split up in 1969. Scruggs had been wanting to do newer country songs, some Bob Dylan too, and Flatt wouldn't go along with it. I was discussing this problem with my banjo teacher, who suddenly got a most uncharacteristic sneer on his face and scoffed, 'Yeah, I heard that Scruggs was a *liberal.*' This chilled me – he was talking about him like he was DEAD! Was my teacher going to *stop playing* Scruggs style merely because of the Vietnam war? That's *Pete*'s department! Indeed there were many dark mutterings about Scruggs's leanings in the redneck depths of the Bay Area music scene – the guys who associated bluegrass with the John Birch Society and the National Rifle Association. Ken and I found ourselves in some scary garages and back yards at the time.

The errors of Flatt and Scruggs

There was a man called Paul Henning, who spent his whole life as a rabid professional cornball. The 'creator' (what a word) of *The Beverly Hillbillies*, a television show remarkable even in 1962 for its fatuousness, a world marker for stupidity, he got Flatt and Scruggs to perform its theme tune, 'The Ballad of Jed Clampett'.

Which then became a stinking musical albatross – everyone wanted to hear them play it instead of their real stuff. This must have been more than a little galling.

Later Henning got Flatt and Scruggs to appear as guests on the show. The plot called for them to serenade Minnie Pearl, a comedienne from the Grand Ole Opry who wore a straw hat with the price tag still on it and purported to bring news from the sticks. Cousin Zeke fell into the well last Thursday . . . Perhaps you have a Grand Ole Opry side. I don't. This tender love song, 'Pearl, Pearl, Pearl', written in haste one imagines, Lester and Earl were obliged to perform many times. Thankfully the law of copyright forbids my quoting it – it's enough, isn't it, to note that it rhymes Scruggs with hugs, and includes references to mules and possum fat. This stuff was embarrassing to us. Flatt and Scruggs were seriously good musicians. They were interested in beauty. And these kinds of ANTICS didn't suit them.

I draw a flour sack over 'Talking Banjo'. The title sounds deceptively Seeger- or Guthrie-esque, though it's a totally undelectable piece of Kentucky HAM. It's a perplexing, irritating number you think is never going to end, and that Flatt was obviously dubious about, in which Scruggs pretended to make his Mastertone 'talk' to him by bending a lot of notes and using his revolutionary 'Scruggs tuners'. First the banjo says it wants its momma and then asks for a drink of water. Fortunately, 'Talking Banjo' seems to have almost disappeared from western civilisation, perhaps digitally suppressed by the Legion of Banjo Decency.

Interlude: Lester Flatt's voice

Bill Monroe said the sound of bluegrass ought to be 'high and lonesome'. True. But you can get too high with it. There are not many professional castrati in Tennessee and Kentucky and I find it hard to imagine that folks there can relate to a lonesome sound approaching registers that only dogs can hear. Monroe, when not at his best, sounds like he's whining. It's like having a raving two-year-old in the house. But Bill Monroe was pure of purpose, and numbers like 'Uncle Pen' and 'In the Pines' are moving pieces of American art.

Flatt's way of singing these songs is much more successful: lonesome, but mellifluous, with an ability to bend some notes in a bluesy way. He flowed the tunes he liked best across the bar lines and what he sang stayed with you, whereas listening to too much Monroe had the same dispiriting effect as keeping a moth in a jar. 'Doin' My Time'. 'Salty Dog Blues'. Flatt's voice was urban but longing for the quiet of a country evening. Or a snowfall in which you lose your fiancée.

Mechanically speaking

The origins of the five-string banjo remain, to me, obscure – the histories are irritatingly vague. (Ken and I thought any music associated with the *four*-string banjo impossibly corny and stupid, which is pretty funny, since most people in the world think that *all* banjos are impossibly corny and stupid.) Somehow the modern instrument with a fairly wide fingerboard arrived in the catalogue of the Gibson company around the middle 1920s. I have never read anything that actually explains how this form of the five-string banjo came to be agreed. The banjo is an extremely technical instrument, not a suggestive or a lyrical one. It is all hard edges – it doesn't exactly invite you to caress it, as does a viola or a guitar. It's like holding a Chrysler on your lap. Or even the Chrysler *Building*. It's really difficult to make such a twanging, clashing hard thing musical. You might as well try to play the 'Largo al Factotum' on the cymbals. There have existed people who could play the five-string banjo, but they are a very small percentage of those who own and operate banjos. Here are their names:

Earl Scruggs

Pete Seeger

That's it. I don't propose to go into the whole awful mess of commercial five-string banjo playing – Roy Clarke, the Stoneman Family, 'Uncle' Dave Macon, 'Grand Pa' Jones, 'Stringbean' . . . the proliferation of quotation marks says it all. Sometimes you wonder why your parents didn't just kill you – I mean this is what I was doing with my life at sixteen, gathering information about a man in silly trousers who called himself Stringbean.

Whatever beginner's banjo we were struggling with, Harmony, Conqueror, or even a banjo from Sears, we all aspired, really, to the Gibson Mastertone, the heavy, solid, high-volume machine Scruggs played. The old Mastertones had a sound you could taste, chew on, dream about. I have never yet acquired a Mastertone, despite becoming a grown-up with the power, you would think, to remortgage the house in order to buy one. However the finest banjo I've ever held in my arms, whispered to, played with an ease and surety and volume which shocked the Hell out of me, as if it were alive, was one made by the Stelling company in Virginia. It shot the notes out like arrows. It was incredibly finely balanced, and dangerous, I thought, like a knife, a sharp, gleaming, $600 sushi knife. It cut through ALL MY BULLSHIT. During the five minutes that it was mine.

An effective head cleaner

One day we were sitting in Ken's bedroom. We had swapped banjos and I was talking about something, or maybe we were trying to sing (it was hard work for us, we would *frown* at each other in the strangest way when struggling to understand harmony). Anyway I suddenly DROOLED on to the head of his banjo, which was made of skin, with a nice folky patina to it. Yes, I must have been trying to sing. The drool cut a perfectly white, clean line through this covetable discolouration. We were both astonished. You would have thought he'd be pissed off as Hell, I mean what if you lent me a viola and I blew my nose into it? But he said he had *wanted* to find a way to clean the head of his banjo for months. Whereas I had thought it looked good and Seegerific, he was wishing that it looked cleaner, more Scruggsian. I protested at his request that I drool over the whole thing. We joked that I (note: *I*) could make a fortune selling this Patent Banjo Head Cleaner, just sitting around all day slobbering into little bottles. Found money. We still make this joke when we get together, or rather *he* does. He was generous about it, but I felt at the time, as you do at sixteen, that this nauseating incident underlined my general physical offensiveness. I was also mortified that, because the head on my banjo was plastic, BECAUSE MY ENTIRE BANJO WAS PLASTIC, it could never *get* discoloured. Merely wipe with damp rag. I was playing a *fake banjo*. Everything plastic is fake – name one plastic thing that is real. But therefore fake banjos will disappear along with the world's oil supply, so at least there's that to look forward to. From the banjo point of view.

In which my banjo is dissed!

I now have the banjo Ken made for me in the 1970s, when he tried his hand at instrument making. It has an assertive crispness to its tone, and the action is everything I used to dream about, along with 'planetary' tuners, woo *hoo*! The peghead is decorated with a spreading tree, inlaid with mother of pearl. A luthier I know, who builds five-string banjos among other things, said to me recently that as anyone who makes a banjo gets his hardware (a banjo is largely ironmongery) from the Stewart-MacDonald company in Athens, Ohio, 'the only thing that can be original is the inlay on the neck'. Several years ago I had occasion to take my banjo to be repaired by some jerk in England. England! – that land of goddamned *unsyncopated* Brit-ass bluegrass! Anyway I was stuck there. I asked him what he thought of it. He strummed it and turned it in his hand. 'Rather crude inlay,' he minced. *Au contraire, salaud.* My banjo has a beautiful vine that twines up and down the fingerboard, just inviting you to play 'Wildwood Flower'. Both of these guys need to be PUNCHED OUT.

I become dapper

When I went to college in New York City, I was not dapper. I was CALLOW. My Seeger side took over. I actually thought of leaving New York and going to the *University of Maine* to study 'fisheries management'. God. Things seemed better in the spring, but when I had a bad day I would *fight Manhattan* with Seeger: a 'Folkways' LP from a furtive-feeling record shop in the Village, or a shirt with sleeves to roll up.

But as an adult, it is impossible to maintain any self-respect as the owner of a BANJO in MANHATTAN. Oh how I have tried: I attended bluegrass nights at an awful pizza and beer joint on Canal Street; most of the pizza and beer was on the floor. When I left this place each time I would *skulk*. And at the opera I used to worry that someone there might identify me – 'I have seen that man playing a banjo and eating a pizza!' – and throw me to the crowd. They're emotional people.

The weight of the thing on the subway – pranking people's

bottoms with it during rush hour. It felt *insulting to Manhattan* to carry a banjo around. It felt wrong to play traditional music in New York. It *is* wrong. It's like making Martinis when camping. No, no – *Boston* became first alluring, then inevitable. This is hard to admit, now. On one of my last nights in New York, bitterly cold, Irving and I passed two freezing girls who were playing 'Rickett's Hornpipe' on their fiddles in a doorway in Yorkville. 'Your future life,' he said.

My big mistake

Boston is the more plausible place in which to pursue the traditional arts. It doesn't matter how you dress in Boston, for one thing. The place is also populated by about 800,000 perpetual student types, one of which I blushingly became. Here I was confronted with the remarkable Joe Val, an Italian tenor typewriter repairman who played mandolin in the style of Bill Monroe and had the best bluegrass band in New England. But in Boston you principally get bombarded, even bludgeoned to death, by pseudo-Irish music. I took up the fiddle. Because of delusions about my ancestry I sought out Scottish tunes, though what I mostly learned were the New England and Appalachian fiddle traditions. *English* fiddle music? I join in the catcalls. That's for Morris men and their wee bells.

I felt deeply Thoreauvian there in my candle-lit room with flannel shirt, down vest and fiddle. What a sap. But cracks appeared in my dedication. Having got acquainted with a local violin maker, I thought instrument repair might make a better livelihood for me (at the time I was working as a typist). But my roommate was disdainful: 'I don't know,' he said, waving his arm dismissively, 'working with your *hands* . . .' *He* was going to be a *biologist*.

My roommates and I gave a party one summer day and invited as performers a quartet of girls who played traditional music, one of whom I had the most heart-rending crush on. She could play a spellbinding version of 'The Full-Rigged Ship'. Everybody was very happy and drinking beer all day, the way you think you can when you're twenty-five. I went out on the rotten old back porch to talk with the girl with the fiddle. I sat on the railing, hooked my feet between the rotten old struts, they gave way, and I fell eight feet on to a concrete path. On my head. I had a gash which was sewed up, and I was told officially that I did not have a concussion, but for a number of days things were peculiar. The small talk had been knocked out of me. At the office I was unable to respond to anything people said. And this was the moment, of course, that I phoned up the fiddle girl, on the *one day off* they gave me from work because I'd *hit my head*, and demanded that she come over to my house to be accompanied by me on banjo. I had always considered fiddle and banjo to be the most spectacular combo. Shortly after she arrived, I realised that I was no good at playing in D. And I couldn't think of anything to say, at all, and she left.

My next big mistake

Banjo led to fiddle led to my immersion, or I should say my *intrusion*, pardon *me*, into the traditional music scene in Scotland. Snootily, I first studied the music of the north-east, the compositions of Nathaniel Gow and J Scott Skinner. 'A very *violinistic* tradition', I would proudly repeat, by which I guess it is meant that someone with a name composed it, and wrote it down, and that it involves some playing above First Position. But I was almost completely at sea with the thing. I would never get out of First Position, which meant that my violin was but a fiddle.

I liked the plucky little tunes of Shetland and Orkney, tunes to which the plucky people of these places pluckily march across their bumpy landscapes. But my Highland fiddle teacher said to me once, through his Glenmorangie, 'It's all very well you coming here and studying our music, but what about *your* tradition, eh? *Your* music?' Well! This was what my Scottish wife and the people of the little 'county town' I was living in would say to me whenever I opened my mouth: WHAT ARE YOU DOING HERE? The answer, essentially, was recuperating. Recuperating from America. I had sailed away from America on my violin as if on a raft.

I once took my fiddle to a fiddling contest in the next town. I think it was Auchtermuchty, but I can't remember because it was so traumatic. I entered in the Beginners category, naturally enough, and I was very nervous. There was hardly anyone there, but I trembled my way through a pipe march, strathspey and reel, and it was pretty terrible. The next week, the *Perthshire Advertiser* reported the results of the contest. I had, technically, won, but they saw fit to write next to my name:

(ONLY ENTRANT).

My Edinburgh violin teacher was violently dismissive of my copy of *Kerr's Merry Melodies for the Violin*, because it's from Glasgow. After I'd been taking lessons for a month or so, he put his hand on my shoulder. 'You,' he said, 'should definitely play by ear.' My fiddle, however, had pointed me in a new direction, that is, I got interested in it as an instrument that pre-dates America, and in the violin repertoire. I finally abandoned myself to listening to music I would never be able to play, but this, for me, was my leap into civilisation.

I give up

Bluegrass pretty much has to stay where it was or it starts to sound silly. Some of the melodic players like Bill Keith and Tony Trischka have contributed a new dynamic, say, but they haven't changed the flavour or the theory. This music is fragile, and of a certain time, and not *necessarily* to be kept alive for commercial purposes. I was talking about this to my friend Sam, who knows nothing about bluegrass, and doesn't want to know. I said it was an iteration of folk music based on the conjunction of several key musicians at a particular time. He said, 'Oh, so it's the bebop of folk.' *Voilà*.

The problem with bluegrass and all commercialised folk music is, really, that the talented musicians aren't playing music they are capable of playing. And that is a shame. If you can play the fiddle, have you ever heard Nathan Milstein play the 'Chaconne' from Bach's *Partita No 2*? If you can sing, if you love to sing, don't you want to see how it feels to sing Puccini?

But fiddle and banjo

My bluster about the origins of bluegrass aside, there *is* something that sounds ancient when a five-string banjo and a fiddle are played together, say 'Crossing the Cumberlands'. Scruggs and Paul Warren sometimes made a riveting duet in this way ('Sally Goodin') and Vic Jordan was always great with a fiddler. Listen to Trischka and Richard Greene play 'Little Rabbit'.

For reasons that may be equally false and unfathomable, the dark, throaty rhythm of this instrumental pairing may evoke the history of American tunes more genuinely than a standard bluegrass or traditional ensemble, or some guy who went to Harvard with his sleeves rolled up, come to that. If there is an American repertory of folk tunes existing from – for the sake of argument – 1600, ignoring that many of these melodies came from the Old World, then hearing them on fiddle and banjo seems perfect. In this particular, haunting sonority there is much of deprivation and loneliness. But there is also the solace of company and of nature: sunlight in trees, creeks, hills, snow, rabbits, deer. That there is no singing reminds you of the nation's vastness.

What is galling is the usual *apology* with which most bands introduce an all-too-brief fiddle and banjo number – something totally, artificially HICK, like: 'We're gonna take a break now and let you hear an ol' tune how our ancestors played it on the ol' front porch, just the fiddle and the ol' banjo . . .' What the hell is he talking about? My 'ancestors' didn't have *porches*! When they start rolling out the 'ol's', I reach for the Steve Reich. But follies and disillusionments aside, to hear 'The Soldier's Joy', 'Cumberland Gap' or 'Cripple Creek' played by a sweet fiddler and a genius banjo player can give you pause. It makes my heart ache for what has become of our republic.

The Day My Sister and I Bought

Sgt Pepper

Living Stereo

Our Dad was one of the pioneers of high fidelity in our county. One Saturday afternoon he put me into the Brown Car and drove far out into the orange groves. There were people living out here in old-fashioned cottages of the 1920s, surrounded with orange trees, flowers, bees. We pulled up at one of these to visit a colleague of Dad's. They were all called Stu. Stu welcomed us into his cottage, which must have been remodelled for the purposes of high fidelity, as there was a spacious, high-ceilinged room, panelled in pine, with a stone fireplace – the room matched Stu's plaid shirt and pipe smoke. Built into one wall was a large hi-fi system, maybe one of the very first – it looked *industrial*. There was a reel-to-reel tape deck, vacuum tube amplifiers and tuners. We stood attentively in this big room while Big Stu went on in a big voice about the big hi-fi. Dad took it all in.

One rainy night we drove to *another town*. We were getting

closer and closer to STEREO. Dad had decided to build his own. This was what all the Stus did, all the young family-men engineers. Dad must have been full of inner joy, even turmoil, about the coming of stereophonic high fidelity, but he kept everything to himself and seemed calm about it. There was a month or two of SOLDERING. He was very neat.

Nobody gives a damn about whether they hear anything *in stereo* any more – they just listen to music from any goddamn angle . . . like before anyone went to the trouble! If you asked most people *why* stereos have two speakers they wouldn't know what the Hell you were talking about. But the road to stereo was a gruelling challenge for the high panjandrums of audio engineering. It involved the deaths of hundreds of nerds, one of the most cruelly ignored of our many twentieth-century massacres, culminating in 1958 with the securing for humanity of the Westrex disc cutter . . .

Don't even talk to me about speaker grille cloth!

The only way to hear the stereophonic effect, according to Stu, was to position your head *precisely* mid-way between the speakers. Stu had a carpenter's measuring tape to the purpose, and had built a *clamp for his head* into his listening armchair. Then you LISTENED, without blinking, with all the lights on. NO TALKING.

These poor men, my own father included, then became the victims of one of the most debased, exploitative industries the world has ever known. The record companies rushed out album after album of mind-bending, harshly delineated stereo, stereo *anything*, which took your helpless, screwed-down head and violated it with the sounds of elephants, steam trains, shimmering, hastily conceived and assembled fifty-harp orchestras, over-produced records in which the recording engineers, drunk with new-found power, panned madly left to right, right to left . . . Not to mention the thousands of LPs of shatteringly bad music overlaid with a craven, silly patina of 'exotica'. Our family possessed a paragon of this genre, *Around the World in Percussion*, 'starring' Irv Cottler. He was a presentable enough guy, to judge from the sleeve, though to me he looked no drummer. Some awful orchestra played pieces like 'In a Persian Market' while Cottler did weird percussive things, sort of *off to the side*, hacking away at timbales, claves, gourds, triangles, Chinese blocks, gongs, cow bells, bongos, congas, pots and pans and his (ick) *Rogers* drum set.

This kind of thing of course got very tiring; Dad made a break for it by starting to collect music from the Baroque, which was undergoing a revival in the 1960s, thanks to labels like Nonesuch and Deutsche Grammophon, which were actually recording music, and not *The 100 Castanets Play Leroy Anderson*. But he and others eventually began to suffer a strange, listless *Baroque overload*. 'This stuff is driving me crazy,' he said one day, 'it's like a goddamn music box. You just crank away and it all comes out the same, deedle eedle deedle eedle . . .' Then he went out and started buying *Herb Alpert*. Hardly fair to Bach.

My doctor told me these early audio experiences have affected me profoundly, though my solicitor said perhaps not quite to the point of being actionable. They are the reason I have in my music collection things like fife and drum albums, records of fairground organs, *cartoon music* – although the funny thing about cartoon music is that there is nothing cartoonish about it. Who *else* was going to give us Rossini? Certainly not the school, where our early music education consisted of being told to lie on the floor with your head on a paper towel and to say out loud what *The Grand Canyon Suite* made you THINK of . . . ? Year upon *year*? And *never* to tap your feet? You have to hand it to Carl Stalling and Bernard Herrmann and the Newmans and all those guys for introducing twentieth-century sonorities to the public, who otherwise would have BOOED them out of existence. If it's in a movie it's OK.

But damage done by the early stereo industry can't be underestimated – all these locomotives and orphaned congas and cuckoo orchestras, to say nothing of the pop chart, the habit of nerdily, obsessively listening to a track over and over again, a chore eventually taken over by AM radio and which colours all male existence. Beware.

To anyone who complained, complains about what happened to music in the 1960s I say **phooey**. Take a good look at what music had become: Perry Como, Tennessee Ernie Ford, Jackie Gleason: *Music, Martinis and Memories*. Herb Alpert and the Tijuana Brass were signalling the END of musical life in America. A lot of eggs were going to have to be broken, what a good album that would have been: *Eggs Being Broken Around the World in Stereo*. The Beatles *et al* HAD to happen, just like the Russian and Chinese revolutions: look at what was there before.

The Day We Bought Sgt Pepper

The family was pottering along OK in 1967. There had been a few deaths to be glossed over, some illnesses which had not turned major. The family was experiencing the same DECORATIVE FEARS, the same uncertainties about which way to go, in the house, and the future, as every other family. Take this spherical, sapphire and seaweed-green, crystal-crumby encrusted ceiling lamp: does it go with American colonial furniture and brown Naugahyde or tartan upholstery? YEAH!

All the parents thought in the late sixties that society was flying apart, before their very eyes. What a wave of empty successes, botched successes, disruptions, assassinations and lots of people just generally getting their asses kicked! Because of all this fear, the parents were living in a completely unreal, magical universe, where every person, thing and idea had a hidden malevolence. In the yellow TV room where our sensational new crusty blue light hung, innovatively illuminating the future, we watched Kennedy after Kennedy get buried. We saw Americans let loose on the moon to no purpose, on a brand-new colour TV which Dad had reverently placed on a very high stand (altar) so that we looked *up* to these events. In this room, if I am not mistaken, my sister smoked her first cigarette; I languished here for weeks one year with a *mystery illness*, which might well have been a profound Fear of the Future. But the first historic schism in which our TV room and crusty lamp participated, along with many other threatened family dens all over America, was the week in 1967 when my sister and I brought *Sgt Pepper's Lonely Hearts Club Band* into the house.

This really was the apocalypse. All the parents must have been pre-warned about the horrendous social corrosiveness of this record; they seemed to fear it as an almost *universal solvent of morals*. They may have been terrorised by our eerily fearful local press, or maybe from *Time* magazine, which in the late 1960s was a schizophrenic grab-bag of occasionally punchy anti-government reporting and (more often) lily-livered, trembling conservatism and xenophobia. Anyway they seemed to get right on the case, sniffing around and demanding to know what it was all about . . . this was it, eh? The literal *sound of degeneracy* they'd been hearing about. Hot diggity! They *totally ruined* the thrill of bringing home a new LP, unwrapping it, smelling it, nervously placing the needle (sorry, the *stylus*) on the first groove . . . like a great date, you peel off the . . .

Two things really bugged them about *Sgt Pepper*: 'She's Leaving Home', which it seemed was a call to all the offspring of the bourgeoisie to run away and shack up with people who couldn't provide for them, and 'A Day in the Life', with its famous *orchestral maelstrom*. Mom told us that it was like *being given a general anaesthetic*, ergo this must be some kind of drug-inveigling shenanigan, not to mention all this talk about turning you on, what the Hell! She hastened to tell us that the 'gigolo' (her word) in the 'motor trade' must have been a *very* déclassé person indeed, as that is what they all were, and she also thought the holes in the Albert Hall were a *very* disrespectful thing, why Prince Albert was a personage everyone in *England* looked up to still. Our Mom was a kind of unofficial English cultural ambassadress to California, just look at our dinnerware.

Dad intoned, 'I think this is a very bad thing the Beatles are doing,' referring also to the girl running away with the string quartet. I thought that he was missing out on the *extreme stereo separation* on this record, carping as he literally was from the sidelines. But, my sister piped up, isn't it just a story? *I* don't want to run away. Her *parents* were upsetting her, not the *Beatles*. Now to bolster their arguments they dragged Grandpa into it (he was staying with us at the time), and what he made of it was impossible to understand, he couldn't even HEAR. But Dad explained very LOUDLY that the Beatles were trying to get us to go *loco in cabeza* and run away with people who were not like us, and Grandpa made the appropriate noises, *clucks* really, all the while trying to adjust his hearing aid. I always listened to him but in this case he'd been tricked into agreeing with my father.

I don't think they were too keen on the masturbatory noises in 'Lovely Rita', or the *sitars*, though a little later, in our FAKE DRUG PERIOD, we were allowed a Ravi Shankar album and incense, *Mysore Sugandhi Dhoop*. In the end Dad stood up and made quite an eloquent speech, in which he asserted and attempted to demonstrate that the Beatles (and Herbert Marcuse) had been responsible for absolutely everything that went wrong in the whole country from 1963 to the present, and all the woes that were to come. (Certainly not people like George Wallace, William Westmoreland, Robert MacNamara, oh *no*. Do you *get* this?) Then he subsided.

'When I'm Sixty-Four' they *liked*! So despite this conniption the day *Sgt Pepper* arrived, they didn't confiscate it, never entirely banned it, just looked perpetually dark about it. The dears.

Sgt Pepper unleashed a tidal wave of marketing crap all over everybody. The search was on for old bandsmen's uniforms, sitars, various agarbattis, dhoops, decorative (?) hookahs. I made some kind of device, the look of which was most highly disapproved of, for our FAKE DRUG PERIOD, from a collection of glass and metal tubing that had previously seen service as my frog-embalming machine.

Much later, my father laid a clipping from the *Wall Street Journal* (of all the—) in front of me. 'One of the Beatles has written a very bitter book,' he said triumphantly. So at least *that* made him happy, for a while. But then again, some years on, he and I were watching something on television which featured a clip of the Beatles from long before, from their MOPTOP period. I looked at him and said, 'Pretty innocuous, huh?' Without looking away from the screen he nodded and very slowly said: Yes.

There is a lot of talk nowadays about waste and chemicals which have destroyed everything, but music destroys a lot more than waste and chemicals do, it is music that will eventually destroy absolutely everything *totally*, mark my words.

THOMAS BERNHARD

Hell! Music became a, *the* drug – something more pernicious than heroin or even petroleum. Americans now live their lives to 'anthems', songs that *seem* to inspire and renew life, *seem* to 'mean something', when in fact they only hypnotise them and degrade their sensibilities. Terrible music convinces them that their actions, whatever they may be, are all right as long as they are back-lit by this infinite commercial howling. Music is making fools of them. Is there any better illustration of Bernhard's fears than the 'thrash rock' perpetually listened to by the brave, very young American tank commanders and bombardiers in Iraq?

When I Become King!

I
ALL PUBLICATIONS REQUIRED TO SWAP NAMES.
To be supervised personally by the King, who believes that
some publications have lasted far too long on the reputation of
their names alone, whereas other publications of good quality
and an industrious nature labour under unfortunate titles. A
name of opposite meaning and intent shall be bestowed on the
publication in question. Exempli gratia: from this day
The New York Times will publish and trade under the name
Naughty Spanking Nurses, and vice-versa. *Similarly,* literary
criticism to be sold only in dirty shops along 42nd Street.

II
GARBAGE AND TRASH TO BE HAND DECORATED.
before being discarded. In at least two colours. The
decoration to be scrutinised by representatives of the
Ministry of Junk.

217

III
AN AGE-OLD WORRY AND NUISANCE ENDED.
No more white pencils, white crayons, or white felt tip pens. Manufacture to cease immediately. The King believes that over 600 billion of these have already been discarded in history. The Ministry of Junk estimates that 75 per cent of His Majesty's landfill sites are white crayons and the white pencils from sets of iffy coloured pencils. The populace to turn in all unused, linty, dusty white crayons etc. to the police for an immediate amnesty and refund. Tailors allowed to keep white chalk under special licence.

IV
FLORIDA.
Politically incorporated into Nevada and physically moved there. His Majesty feels it was time.

V
THE END OF FRUSTRATION. READING.
Strictly prohibited now to have an asterisk in any text, book, newspaper, or advertisement, to which the reference cannot be found. Similarly any index in a book, hardback OR paperback, in which the page numbers do not correlate with the text. The relevant author, editor, typesetter, printer and proprietor to be denied computers in perpetuity, given rusty typewriters and sent to Seattle.

VI
SAFER HIGHWAYS.

No 'vanity' licence plates may be employed which are 'in' jokes or not readily understandable by other drivers. The Ministry of Stupidity estimates 90 per cent of traffic accidents in the Kingdom last year were caused by drivers puzzling over plates such as BXB 4NUT KUFFYA.

VII
THE WOMAN.

at the wheel of a red Jaguar who nearly ran over the King at the corner of Santa Cruz Avenue and El Camino Real, Menlo Park, California, on October 9, 1992, juggling a lit cigarette, a mobile phone, a cocktail and a tiny white dog TO BE PAINTED BLUE.

VIII
TO BE ISSUED FREE OF CHARGE.

Transit fares, museum entries, health care, wine, beer, tampons, shaving materials.

IX
TELEVISION.
Nah.

X
MOTOR CARS.
What do YOU think?

XI
NO DOCU DRAMA.
Production to cease immediately. As of today there are only *documentary* and *drama*. Biopics to be strictly controlled by the Media Department of the Ministry of Stupidity. Loni Anderson to be taken under Government protection in the Identity Erasure Scheme. Oprah Winfrey ordered to surrender within thirty days.

XII
BALANCE IN LIFE.
Anyone who jogs *or* regularly attends a gymnasium for the express purpose of 'staying in shape' now required to smoke twenty cigarettes per day. His Majesty's object: balance in personal life and also in the economy.

XIII
NO DOLLS.

XIV
NO PHONY RUSSIAN LETTERING.
or Chinesey alphabets allowed in advertisements for plays, books, restaurants. Insertion of a reversed 'R' in an otherwise

English word to make it look Russian will result in the letters in
the offender's name being permanently reversed, along with his
FACE. *Similarly,* 'Helvetica' and 'Souvenir' type faces no more.
These eras did not happen. Also the King wants fewer logotypes
and *expressly forbids* logotypes fusing letters together in two
different shades of the same colour.

XV
NO CLOTHING THAT SAYS ANYTHING.

XVI
WHITE MEN. BUSINESS.

White men are no longer allowed to run businesses. They will be
put in a conservation corps and not allowed to leave the woods.
Ever.

XVII
STAR TREK

and *Star Wars* negatives to be kept in the same room with the
last remaining smallpox viruses at the Centers for Disease
Control. No admission.

XVIII
WINE. TALK.

Those who would speak of wine must hold a degree in oenology
from a French university and carry it on their person at all times.
Everyone else to shut the Hell up about it.

XIX
JAPAN.

The Japanese to have the only standing army on the planet, expressly *for the defence of the planet*. They are armed with beautiful swords.

T McE R e x.

The Elk's Funeral

Some Elks Lodges glitter like country clubs; this one used to be a motel with pancake house attached. In the parking lot, stretching after the hot drive, there is a pretty girl in a black dress. Not one of you. But she must be, no one but your party is wearing black to the Elks Club at three o'clock today, in eighty degree weather.

The bar your only foyer. It's filled with smoke, hugely, by a few afternoon drunks. After all, the Elks raised themselves in the face of the Temperance movement, so that men might drink. A hundred years ago. Skewed portraits of fly-blown guys, the officers, look down at you. They are photographed at odd angles, as though they were wearing party hats, but they aren't; as if the hot parking lot sunlight you've just admitted yelled HEY SHUT UP YOU GUYS and they're chastened, maybe even a little ashamed. Most of them sport big glasses from mall opticians above their plump, sallow cheeks. A woman of sixty stands by the guest book. Suddenly, you recognise her. His first wife.

A Calvert Reserve blackboard both points and blocks the way to the service. You walk by acres of tables set for dinner. Not his, not ours. The glasses are clean and the napkins starched; there are cigarette butts in the corners. The big ballroom of acoustical tile and old linoleum. You push the people gathering here into the few identities you know. By her severely drawn eyebrows you find Sallie, by the hairline receding even in youth you guess Herb. But where is the remembered suntan, the back that was once so straight? One fluorescent light is giving up the ghost where the ceiling is damp. An exit door stumblingly enjoins the brothers NO DRINKS IN THE PARKING LOT, yes, Elks know when to leave it be. As their departed brother has done.

Against each wall stands an ornate throne, junk, dark Victorian junk, pulled by crowbar from the old lodge, twenty years ago, in the doomed downtown. Sitting on each is a battered-looking Elk in a frayed tuxedo or black suit, his shoes cracked as the skin around his eyes. You feel sure they will sleep, and soon. They wear silver chains about their necks, which makes them look like sommeliers. An ornate table, also of the past glories of the lodge, on this dirty flooring. Flowers and a few family pictures. Your uncle young, in his uniform. *Come sit with us, in the family chairs,* says the second wife. *Don't introduce us,* says your father, *we're not really related.*

Even now, here, you are going to try to sidle away from death?

The chief wine waiter, the Exalted Ruler, flushed from leaving an office which looks very like this, rises and begins. First a bible will be presented to the widow. In a royal blue suit, perhaps a tuxedo demoted for bad behaviour, a little man gets up. *I didn't know our brother long, but you could set your watch by him. Every day at three o'clock I'd have his glass of wine on the bar, with his little straw in it, and in he'd come. There was a lotta wisdom coming out of that man, a lotta wisdom. And it's my pleasure to be able to present this bible to his widow. And thank you all.* He hands her the bible, in a cedar souvenir-ware chest. Bemusement of the guests, supplanted by the realisation that his sons have *asked* the barman to speak. Later, driving home in the valley, you're moved by this. From miserable thoughts of this bible in its Trees of Mystery box, you turn with a jolt to his third wife's genuine grief. And it is not the grief you are selfishly feeling, what if *your* funeral were to be like this. She is mourning her husband.

Now we are gifted a look at the mysteries of the Elks, when they are at their most vulnerable. Behind the words of the service, which might have been written by Sinclair Lewis on a bender, behind the lamely intoned honorifics, Exalted Ruler, Recording Knight, you hear Art Carney's voice, faint, filled not with satire but with precisely the solemnity of Elks and Masons and Moose, all these people who know there exists something noble, something mysterious, something *important about something*, but do not know what it is or how to find it.

The Recording Knight stands up and in his best Kent filtered, Calvert reserved voice calls the name of our departed brother. Alas, he can answer no more, he has passed into the shadows. He is not at the bar either. He is in the Lodge of Sorrow. The Exalted Ruler, who has his own parking space, invites us to listen to the tolling of eleven hours on the great Clock of Elkdom, which begins to bong like a doorbell when he touches a button. The hour of eleven is the hour of remembrance for all Elks, when the great heart of Elkdom swells and throbs. Sprigs of ivy will now be placed on the table, ivy the symbol to all Elks that brotherhood is undying, and the Exalted Ruler shakes his head, no no, you guys are coming forward with your plastic sprigs before your cue. Their sense of lodge ritual has not been out of bed at three in the afternoon for some time.

The Exalted Ruler calls for spontaneous testimonials and remembrances. A man gets up, gives his name, says he'll never forget him. A woman was at his birthday party in the fourth grade. All those years ago. And, silence. Especially from the hard-bitten Elks in their section, who would be raising the first drinks with him now. Most are thinking too hard, derailed by the flashing clock, to muster a clear idea of their departed brother. Somebody lights a cigarette. This lack of words for him and the second wife breaks down, recovers herself – after all, what does one say? *He helped my children. He used to have a few drinks. He gave me some folders about Guadalajara.* All of this is beside the point.

People get up and smile. The janitor begins replacing the big ceremonial furniture of the lodge; it's mounted on castors. He looks around at all the chairs he set up, and the flowers. You can see beer and a cigar in his eye. Over the altar (bible, flag and antlers) there hangs a large glass star, suspended from an electric motor. You catch your pretty cousin's eye – you're both guessing its role in mysteries you will not know. *Come on over to the house,* says the third wife. *It's not far.*

In a house dimly remembered you look at each other, you who have not spoken or seen one another for twenty years. Your insurance cousin has been schooled in drink by the deceased. Your policeman cousin tensely displays his pectoral development under his off-duty jacket. And your young bicycling cousin, now grey and a grandfather.

What did he die of? *He thought he had cancer.* What did the doctor say? *He didn't go to the doctor. He didn't have it, but he died.* No one has had much of anyone's news. Mistakes are made but of course forgiven. *The restaurant burned down in 1987. I'm selling carpet tile. It's all 'Red Lobster' around here now, there's no future for fine dining in this valley.*